Museums as Agents
of Change

AMERICAN ALLIANCE OF MUSEUMS

The American Alliance of Museums (AAM) has been bringing museums together since 1906, helping to develop standards and best practices, gathering and sharing knowledge, and providing advocacy on issues of concern to the entire museum community. Representing more than 35,000 individual museum professionals and volunteers, institutions, and corporate partners serving the museum field, the Alliance stands for the broad scope of the museum community.

The American Alliance of Museums' mission is to champion museums and nurture excellence in partnership with its members and allies.

Books published by AAM further the Alliance's mission to make standards and best practices for the broad museum community widely available.

Museums as Agents of Change

A Guide to Becoming a Changemaker

Mike Murawski

ROWMAN & LITTLEFIELD

Lanham • Boulder • New York • London

Published by Rowman & Littlefield
An imprint of The Rowman & Littlefield Publishing Group, Inc.
4501 Forbes Boulevard, Suite 200, Lanham, Maryland 20706
www.rowman.com

6 Tinworth Street, London SE11 5AL, United Kingdom

British Library Cataloguing in Publication Information Available

Library of Congress Cataloging-in-Publication Data

Names: Murawski, Michael, 1977– author. | American Alliance of Museums, issuing body.
Title: Museums as agents of change : a guide to becoming a changemaker / Michael Murawski.
Description: Lanham : Rowman & Littlefield, [2021] | Includes bibliographical references and index.
Identifiers: LCCN 2020054142 (print) | LCCN 2020054143 (ebook) | ISBN 9781538108949 (cloth) | ISBN 9781538108956 (paperback) | ISBN 9781538108963 (epub)
Subjects: LCSH: Museums and community. | Social action.
Classification: LCC AM7 .M77 2021 (print) | LCC AM7 (ebook) | DDC 069—dc23
LC record available at https://lccn.loc.gov/2020054142
LC ebook record available at https://lccn.loc.gov/2020054143

To my son Holden.
May we always be changing, learning,
and working toward a better, more loving future.

Contents

Acknowledgments

For me, writing a book like this has been a journey that could not have been possible without so many other people. As I write these pages of gratitude, I am thinking of the words of educator and organizer Mariame Kaba: "Everything worthwhile is done with other people." Nothing could be more true. Rather than isolated individuals striving to achieve our own greatness in this world, we are all parts of intricate networks of human relationships. Our ideas, inspirations, and creativity flow out from this river of inseparable interconnection, and we all owe immense gratitude to those around us—near and far—throughout our lives. While the list of people who have had a role in shaping my ideas, beliefs, and values is far longer than could ever fit in these pages, I want to recognize many of those whose guidance and patience helped make this book become a thing you are now holding in your hands.

Across the past twenty years, I have had the privilege of working with some of the most amazing and dedicated educators, artists, museum professionals, community organizers, and leaders. Among the hundreds of individuals that I'm proud to have worked alongside and with over the years, I want to celebrate a few that continue to stand out to me right now as I put the finishing touches on this book project.

I want to thank Cheryl Benjamin, who always made me a better educator and a better human being; Monica Montgomery, who has always taught me to be tenacious and to stand up for what I believe in; Rika Burnham and Elliott Kai-Kee, who guided my first great museum experience one summer many years ago at the Art Institute of Chicago and have always been such strong mentors; La Tanya S. Autry, who has challenged and helped shape so many of my ideas about the transformation needed in museums right now; Nina Simon, who has always helped me become a stronger thinker and a more rebellious changemaker; Stephanie Parrish, who got me into this museum thing to begin with; and Teressa Raiford, who showed me that museums can be so much more than they are. I am grateful for all my teachers, guides, and mentors over the years, and to those who continue to guide and support me.

I also want to thank all those who also agreed to be part of the conversations and dialogues that have been included in this book: Nina Simon, La Tanya S. Autry, Lori Fogarty, Lauren Ruffin, Molly Alloy, Nathanael Andreini, and Monica Montgomery. So much of what I have learned about changing museums has been in conversation with others, and it has been important to me that this book honor that process of dialogue and shared discovery.

I want to thank each and every individual who has contributed to ArtMuseumTeaching.com over the past ten years. This site began as simply a space for me to share my own passion for museum teaching, and it grew into a thriving community of educators, thinkers, and change leaders who see the potential of museums as spaces of experimentation, connection, community, equity, care, and belonging. This book would not be possible without everyone who has contributed to and supported this site over the years.

I am grateful to my editor, Charles Harmon, for his guidance, and to the entire team at Rowman & Littlefield Publishing and the American Alliance of Museums for being willing to support me and help me get my ideas out into the world.

My deep thanks go to my family. To my dad who has always been there for me, and to my mom whom I know is looking down on me with immense pride. I am walking down this path right now thanks to my parents who helped set my course.

To my wife and partner in life, Bryna. Without your patience, love, and support, I would not be writing this book. You have put up with so many conversations about museums, and you've challenged my ideas in ways that make me stronger. You have shaped who I am, what I believe in, and my passion to stand up and speak out for what is right. I am so grateful to be on this journey with you.

Finally, to my son Holden. This book is for you. Always remember to stand up and speak out, too, for what you believe in. I know you are going to be a part of making this world a better place.

Preface

Museums as Agents of Change

Museums everywhere have the potential to serve as agents of social change—bringing people together, contributing to local communities, and changing people's lives. Yet, for far too many institutions, this potential continues to go largely untapped. Many museum leaders and professionals remain ambivalent about the social responsibilities of museums and uncertain about the capacity of museums to function as agents of positive change in society. Given the ongoing pandemic and our current moment of continued political polarization, highly contested social debates, and widespread global efforts to confront oppression, now is the time to challenge the entrenched traditional notions of museums and proactively shape a new future.

I think in moments like these, it's important for all of us—whether you work for a museum or not—to pause and reflect on the roles that these institutions serve within our communities. Yes, museums are largely institutions that hold, preserve, and exhibit objects and collections. But they are also living institutions that serve a powerful role as active spaces for connection and coming together; for dialogue and difficult conversations; for listening and sharing; and for care, healing, and repair. Museums have the potential to tell new and diverse histories; amplify marginalized voices; celebrate unheard stories; and recognize the creativity, knowledge, expertise, and lived experience that is already thriving within their local communities. They can be spaces for acknowledging and reflecting on difference, and for bridging divides. They can be spaces for justice, growth, struggle, love, and hope. Now is the time for us to become changemakers and realize the potential of museums as transformative spaces of human connection, care, listening, and deep learning.

So how can we, as individuals, radically expand the work of museums? How can we more fiercely recognize the meaningful work that museums are doing to enact change around the relevant issues in our communities? How can we work together to create change within museums and make a bigger difference in society? Questions like these are increasingly vital for all museum professionals to consider, no matter what your role is within your institution. These questions are also important for all of us to think about more deeply as citizens and community members. This book is about the work we need to do—as museum professionals, visitors, civic leaders, community organizers, and the broader public—to become changemakers and demand that our museums take action toward positive social change and bring people together into a more just, equitable, compassionate, and connected society. It is a journey toward tapping the energies within all of us to make change happen.

WHAT DOES IT MEAN FOR MUSEUMS TO BE AGENTS OF CHANGE?

On May 27, 2017, the Portland Art Museum in Portland, Oregon, hosted its first-ever Upstanders Festival, a day of spoken word performances, music, interactive workshops, and art making in support of social justice activism and positive community change. Produced by the Monica Montgomery and Museum of Impact in partnership with Don't Shoot Portland, the festival was part of a series of programs I helped develop to expand community ownership and bring communities of color into the work of co-creating programs at the museum. Just hours before the festival was set to kick off, a white supremacist fatally stabbed two people and injured a third after he was confronted for shouting racist and anti-Muslim slurs at two teenage girls on a MAX Light Rail train here in Portland—less than four miles from the art museum.

Rather than canceling the festival in light of this shocking and horrific attack, we were more committed than ever to open the museum as a place for people to come together as a community and to engage with the arts in ways that celebrate difference and build empathy, dialogue, and understanding. Teressa Raiford, community organizer and founder of Don't Shoot Portland, later remarked how much the museum felt like a sanctuary that day. Another artist involved in the workshops and activities of the festival, Karina Puente, also reflected on how a program like this gave the Portland community "a place to heal." The art, music, dialogue, and energy of the Upstanders Festival brought more than eight hundred people together at the museum that day—just hours after the traumatic attack—to stand together against hate, discrimination, and violence.

Events and partnerships just like the Upstanders Festival have occurred at many museums across the country, pushing these institutions beyond being just a collection of objects. These museums are working toward being agents of positive change, acting upon the inequalities within and outside their local communities as well as contributing to a more just, equitable, and connected world. It is essential to recognize that becoming an agent of change does not happen because of a single event or project, and it certainly does not happen alone. The transformation happening right now at so many museums is the result of the passionate dedication of staff across departments as well as a rapidly growing network of community partners and so many individuals dedicated to making change happen. This work involves an enormous amount of listening, developing trust, and building relationships—both within a museum as well as with its audiences and communities. It involves understanding the human-centered role of museums, defining what *community* truly means for an institution, and shaping a set of core values that reflect a commitment to accessibility, inclusion, justice, and human rights. It involves rethinking power dynamics and ideas of leadership. It involves developing practices of care and healing, and growing a community of change to do this work together. And, last but not least, it involves a lot of love. Love for museums, and love that emerges among the relationships we build throughout this changemaking process.

There is considerable consensus among scholars about the core social responsibilities of museums, yet the idea of museums as agents of social change is still a contested and uncomfortable proposition for many institutions, their directors, their boards of trustees, and even across the field of museums as a whole. In the work that I've been involved in shaping museums, there has been no easy pathway to making change happen. Each collaboration, partnership, and project presents new barriers and requires creative thinking, persistence, and passionate resolve, from museum staff as well as members of our communities. There is a lot to be learned from our experiences as changemakers and the challenges, tensions, and dynamic collaborations we encounter along the way, which is why I repeatedly reflect on my own experiences throughout this book as well as the challenges faced by others advancing this practice. At the end of the day, becoming a changemaker is about taking risks, sticking to your core values, doing good work, and converting talk into action.

BECOMING CHANGEMAKERS

So how do we start to make a bigger difference? How do we more fiercely recognize and support the meaningful work that museum professionals are already leading to support open dialogues around the challenging, relevant issues of our time? And how do we radically expand this work to build a stronger culture of equity and social justice within museums—one that measures future success through our capacity to bring people together, respond to local realities, foster conversations, and contribute to strong and resilient communities?

This book is about embracing our role as changemakers, taking these principles seriously, and recognizing the essential need for museums to lead and take action rather than just follow, react to, and reflect the times in which we live. Throughout the following chapters, I set out to explore the work of museums as human-centered and community-centered institutions, discussing successes and challenges from a range of institutions doing this work as well as my own experiences as a changemaker. Throughout each chapter, I explore key issues for advancing change within museums as well as practical strategies for making this change happen. I hope that these pages can become a resource and guidebook for those stepping up to become changemakers in their own institutions and communities, providing questions for personal reflection, critically analyzing the work of museums, and reimagining the future of museums.

While writing this book, I was reminded of how important my conversations with other changemakers have been to my own thinking about museums. My ideas exist in dialogue with so many others. Therefore, I have included several meaningful conversations within the pages of this book to honor this process of dialogue and the learning we do collectively and collaboratively. These conversations bring in leading voices in the field of museums and nonprofits to address key issues related to museum transformation and our roles as changemakers. At the beginning of each conversation chapter, I have highlighted a few key ideas that we can bring into our own process of becoming and being changemakers.

Chapter 1 begins by expanding on the idea of a human-centered approach toward museum practice, inviting us to consider the essential value of building relationships and connections across museum communities. This "people first" mindset is an important foundation for becoming a changemaker and cultivating a sense of personal agency in this work. Chapter 2 takes a deeper dive into how we define the concept of "community," and identifies ways to break down barriers between museums and their communities as well as build relevance through local community partnerships. As changemakers, it's important to bring community into the core of our practice and have a thoughtful, clear sense of what that means for ourselves and our institutions. In chapter 3, we hear these ideas come alive through my conversation with museum leader and changemaker Nina Simon, who reflects on her team's work at the Santa Cruz Museum of Art and History, building relationships and recognizing the assets within our local communities.

Becoming changemakers means fighting for an equity-based transformation in museums, and chapter 4 examines white dominant culture and white supremacy as one of the single greatest barriers to the change needed in museums today. Learning to identify our own role in these systems of oppression and working to dismantle racism within museums are both key actions for those advocating for change. Through a conversation with La Tanya S. Autry about our work with the Museums Are Not Neutral initiative, chapter 5 discusses ideas of collective action, mutual aid, and building networks of changemakers through social media activism in the work of erasing the oppressive myth of neutrality in museum culture.

Chapter 6 turns to a focus on leadership and the need for changemakers to challenge conventional ideas about what it means to be a leader and reflect on the values and skills that are truly necessary to shape the future of museums. Through this chapter, I explore ideas of human-centered leadership and collaborative leadership, offering key strategies for making change happen within institutional structures and workplace culture. This chapter is followed by two conversations with changemakers who occupy director or co-director positions in museums and arts nonprofit organizations. First, in chapter 7, I talk with Lori Fogarty, director and CEO of the Oakland Museum of California, about her efforts to shift organizational structures and advocate for a focus on social impact. Then, chapter 8 explores the possibilities of collaborative leadership through a conversation with the co-directors of the Five Oaks Museum, Molly Alloy and Nathanael Andreini, and co-CEO at Fractured Atlas, Lauren Olivia Ruffin.

The final three chapters of this book bring attention to the urgent need for changemakers to develop a practice of care and adopt a mindset of healing within museum institutions. The work of being an agent of change is not easy, and chapter 9 addresses how changemakers can resist the culture of burnout by embracing healing justice in their lives and workplaces. Chapter 10 shares a conversation with museum leader and curator Monica Montgomery about community care and centering an architecture of empathy, advocacy, and social responsibility in our work as leaders of change. The concluding chapter ends with a daring call for us as changemakers to see love—yes, love—as a driving force and core value in the unending work to radically transform museums.

At its core, this book is about our work, individually and collectively, as changemakers to ensure that these institutions live up to their potential to bring people together, build a more equitable future, and change people's lives. I hope something you read in these pages sparks new thinking and new questions, and I look forward to the conversations with many of you about the ideas presented here. Throughout these pages, I also want to reach outside the museum profession and embrace the important role we *all* play in demanding, creating, and supporting the change we need to see happen in museums. These conversations and actions cannot take place solely behind museum walls or in the isolation of professional conferences and existing networks. We need to work together to realize the full potential of museums and discover how a human-centered focus on social action can transform your practice, your museum, and your community.

Let's be a part of making this change happen together!

1

Museums Are Us

Let's start by making an important foundational point about how we talk about museums. When we talk about them more as buildings or brick-and-mortar institutions, it becomes easier to distance ourselves from the human-centered work we do. So it's absolutely essential to remember that museums are made of people: directors, board members, donors, curators, educators, front of house staff, registrars, conservators, security guards, volunteers, maintenance and facilities workers, members, visitors, and community partners. Museums are us.

I am reminded of this by Anna Cutler, director of learning at the Tate Museums in the United Kingdom, whose insightful 2013 Tate Paper titled "Who Will Sing the Song? Learning Beyond Institutional Critique" discussed institutional critique and cultural learning in art museums. In it, she quotes artist Andrea Fraser: "Every time we speak of the 'institution' as other than 'us' we disavow our role in the creation and perpetuation of its conditions" (Cutler 2013). Fraser's work as an artist explores forms of institutional critique that problematize the museum as a complex social site, a view that can be expanded upon as we envision our role as changemakers in museums. Thinking about a museum as the monolithic "it" might make it easier to criticize from the outside; yet gaining an understanding of a museum as "us" certainly sparks a direct sense of the possibility of change from within as well as a clear sense of responsibility for those working in and with museums. As the people involved in the work of a museum, we have a responsibility to understand our role in the system of policies, practices, and power dynamics as well as our ability to change that system.

This is an important basis for any discussion of museums and change because it defines the vision, mission, and work of a museum as the vision, mission, and work of *the people* who are part of that museum. So if we say "museums must be more connected to their communities," we're really talking about what the people who make up the museum need to focus on—being more connected to our communities. We are inseparable from the institution, in other words. Any critique of museums is a critique of the people working for them and making decisions for them; and any change needing to happen in museums is, therefore, a change that needs to start with the people. As part of thinking about museums as made of people, we can work toward identifying those people creating barriers to change and learn to navigate those situations with a greater sense of empathy that can drive action. On the flip side, museum professionals—as change agents and activists within these institutions—have the ability to break down institutional hierarchies and create communities of change across these people-centered networks. We are the change we want to see in museums.

This chapter establishes the human-centered approach toward museums as the foundation of our work as changemakers, inviting us to consider the essential value of building relationships and connections across our museum communities. The following pages will help you examine the importance of a people-centered institution that cultivates empathy and personal agency, and include a series of strategies for changemakers working to implement this shift in mindset within an institution.

AN ECOSYSTEM OF PEOPLE

Thinking about a museum as a connected, human-centered endeavor can sound like common sense. I first personally embraced this idea after having one of those "light bulb" moments early in my career while reading the work of philosopher and educational reformer John Dewey. I had attended the 2007 Teaching Institute in Museum Education, a weeklong intensive professional development experience at the Art Institute of Chicago led by Rika Burnham and Elliott Kai-Kee. During this unforgettable week in the galleries of the Art Institute, we discussed theories of gallery teaching, we had memorable experiences with art, and we talked *a lot* about John Dewey. I had been familiar with Dewey in my graduate studies in teaching and educational theory when "learning by doing" was the mantra of the day. Yet I did not begin to more deeply explore his writings about art and aesthetics until this particular week in Chicago. We read Dewey's writings; met with renowned Dewey scholar Philip Jackson; and, most important, had a range of intellectual, emotional, and collective experiences that opened art up to the rich complexity of our lives. We were enacting the words of Dewey:

The task is to restore continuity between the refined and intensified forms of experience that are works of art and the everyday events, doings, and sufferings that are universally recognized to constitute experience. (Dewey 2005, 3)

I left that week in Chicago with two things that radically changed my career and my personal vision for museums. First, I gained two lifelong mentors in Rika and Elliott, as well as many friendships with colleagues with whom I stay connected to this day. Second, I left with a relentless passion for seeing art as a catalyst for human connection and shared experience, and understanding that we need to bring our whole selves into museum spaces and open ourselves to these experiences. From that moment forward, it seemed clear to me that museums existed to fulfill this goal to realize the true potential of creating connections among a broad ecosystem of people. People to experience, observe, perceive, wonder, feel, question, learn, respond, create, challenge, inspire, and share. People to light up the spaces of museums with energy, emotion, love, hope, and our intrinsic drive to connect with other people through our lived experiences.

Since this initial spark for me back in 2007, I have grown to more deeply understand the essential role of those who are working to make change happen and see museums as spaces of connection and catalysts for social change. I've seen museums become spaces for challenging questions to be asked, for people to question their assumptions, for marginalized voices to shine, and for communities to heal. I've seen museums embrace these human elements at their core and truly take steps toward changing people's lives.

As commonsensical and straightforward as it sounds to think about museums as people- and human-centered institutions, this idea has faced a legacy of rather fierce opposition grounded in outdated traditions and histories. How many museums have mission statements that prioritize the colonizing actions of "collecting" and "preserving" objects, rather than foregrounding the people-centered work of building community, growing empathy and understanding, celebrating human creativity, and cultivating engaged citizenship? How often do museum leaders and boards make decisions that value objects and collections over staff, volunteers, and museum visitors? (We have certainly seen this happen after the pandemic with the museum cuts and staff layoffs that followed.) What if museum leaders and professionals considered human relationships and human impact, first and foremost, when making decisions about exhibitions, interpretation, programs, facilities, policies, and practices? Embracing a human-centered mindset in museums asks us to do just that, advancing compassion, human potential, care, and collective well-being as elements integral to our institution's values and culture. As changemakers, we have a lot of work to do to continue advocating for this mindset within museums.

MUSEUMS IN A SOCIAL WORLD

One definite force sparking a shift toward a social and human-centered mindset for museums and other organizations has been the rise of social media and its influence on behavior across our society. At the core of the continual shift into a more digital age has been new ways of relating to one another; new ways of interacting; new kinds of groups; and new ways of sharing, learning, collaborating, and connecting. In their book *Networked: The New Social Operating System*, Lee Rainie and Barry Wellman argued that the large online social circles of familiar platforms such as Facebook and Twitter actually expand opportunities for learning, problem solving, and personal interaction. Their work at the Pew Internet Project, NetLab, and the Connected Lives Project suggests that digital technologies are not isolated—or isolating—systems, but rather networked systems built upon these social networking platforms as well as mobile device technologies.

> People's relationships remain strong—but they are networked. Neighbors, and neighborhoods still exist, to be sure, but they occupy a smaller portion of people's lives. It is hard to borrow a cup of sugar from a Facebook friend 1,000 miles away, but it has become easier to socialize, get advice, and exchange emotional support at whatever distance. Where commentators had been afraid that the internet would wither in-person ties, it is clear that they enhance and extend them. (Rainie and Wellman 2012, 255)

This extended potential for human connection is certainly something that most museums have embraced for more than a decade, launching into social media platforms in ways that connect to new online audiences across the globe. Beyond simply implementing digital technologies or using social media, museums engaging in digital transformation have been challenged to rethink notions of place, community, and culture in response to the changing behavior and demands of users—digital and analog. In her book *Museums in the Digital Age*, Susana Smith Bautista writes:

> If museums are to remain relevant, vital, and meaningful, then they must adapt to a changing society, which means not only recognizing and incorporating new digital tools for communication, but more importantly, recognizing the changing needs and aspirations of society as reflected in their communities of physical and virtual visitors. (Bautista 2014, 225)

As the behaviors and needs of our audiences change as a result of digital technologies and social media, so do the ways in which they connect with each other. Embracing a mindset of openness, participation, and social connectivity allows museums the chance to extend the boundaries of what is possible, and serve as sites for profound human connection in the twenty-first century. In their book *Humanize: How People-Centric Organizations Succeed in a Social World*, Jamie Notter and Maddie Grant discuss their ideas for developing a more human organization in a world affected by social media and the internet.

> We need organizations that are more human. We need to re-create our organizations so that the power and energy of being human in our work life can be leveraged. This has the power not only to transform our individual experiences in the work world, but also to access untapped potential in our organizations. (Notter and Grant 2011, 4)

Through his work in digital engagement and social innovation in the museum sector, Jasper Visser has explored the connections between museums and this concept of a social business. In his paper "From Social Media to a Social Museum," Visser cites the Social Business Forum in defining a social business as "an organization that has put in place the strategies, technologies, and processes to systematically engage all the individuals in its ecosystem (employees, customers, partners, suppliers) to maximize the co-created value" (Visser 2013, 1). The model of a social business, therefore, focuses on building relationships and connections among its entire community, or ecosystem of people. For museums, this goes beyond just being visitor-centered and means thinking about staff and volunteers as well as neighbors and residents of our communities—all part of an institution's interconnected ecosystem. As Visser states, "[M]useums and most other cultural institutions are inherently social organizations to begin with. They have always thrived on intimate relations with all individuals involved in the joint creation of value" (Visser 2013, 7). This concept of a social museum relies on each and every stakeholder working together toward change, value, and impact. The key elements of a social organization—embracing networks of people, considering social relationships inside and outside the organization, and enhancing collaboration in a way that crosses traditional boundaries—are all core to developing a human-centered mindset in museums and establishing a foundation for the people-powered change work needed in museums.

THE POWER OF HUMAN CONNECTION

Another pivotal force defining this human-centered mindset for museum change is driven by new research and writing on empathy and human connection. These elements are integral to any vision of change for museums, and they are key to the work of transforming museums into places that feel alive with the spirit of connection.

"We are in more urgent need of empathy than ever before," writes Roman Krznaric, author of *Empathy: Why It Matters, and How to Get It* (2014) and founder of the Empathy Library (Delaney 2016). Krznaric is among a growing chorus of voices who see an urgent need for empathy and human understanding in an era too often marked by violence, hatred, resentment, self-interest, and toxic political and social debates. In his TEDx Talk "How to Start an Empathy Revolution," he defines empathy as "the art of stepping into the shoes of another person and looking at the world from their perspective. It's about understanding the thoughts, the feelings, the ideas and experiences that make up their view of the world" (Krznaric 2013).

In September 2015, Krznaric put these ideas into practice in the realm of museums with the development of the Empathy Museum, dedicated to helping visitors develop the skill of putting themselves in others' shoes. Its first exhibit, "A Mile in My Shoes," did quite literally that, setting up in a shoe shop where visitors are fitted with the shoes of another person, invited to walk a mile along the riverside while being immersed in an audio narrative of this stranger's life, and then write a short story about it. With contributions ranging from a sewer worker to a sex worker, the stories covered different aspects of life, from loss and grief to hope and love.

Developing empathy has the potential to create radical social change, "a revolution of human relationships," Krznaric states (Krznaric 2015). His work with the Empathy Museum is but one small example of the types of civically engaged, human-centered practices that have been instituted in an effort to expand the role that museums serve in building empathy and human connection in our communities. Staff working for museums across the globe are launching new efforts to bring people together, facilitate open dialogue, and elevate the voices and stories of marginalized groups to promote greater understanding.

One exceptional example of bringing this approach to empathy and connection into museums is the Multaqa project, which was launched in 2015 by Berlin's state museums. The award-winning project invites refugees from Iraq and Syria to serve as Arabic-speaking tour guides. The project title, *Multaqa*, means "meeting point" in Arabic. The tours are designed to give refugees and newcomers access to the city's museums and facilitate the interchange of diverse cultural and historical experiences. Through this project, the museum is able to surrender part of its authority to the participating refugees, who choose objects for their tours as catalysts of dialogue and reflection. "The point is to allow people to use the space for themselves, with their own approaches, with their own questions," says Stefan Weber, the director of the Museum für Islamische Kunst in Berlin. "Having to open up has shown us that we have yet more very different opportunities for developing our relevance to people, if they are asked to join in the discussion and contribute their own realities to it" (Bahr-Reisinger 2016).

In their book *Cities, Museums, and Soft Power*, Gail Dexter Lord and Ngaire Blankenship discuss the human social behaviors of *bridging* and *bonding* that museums have the distinct potential to promote and amplify, especially through public programs, education, and exhibitions.

> Museums and cities have a strong role to play together in bridging and bonding. They bring people together at similar life stages . . . or with identity in common . . . where they can share their experiences. Museums also bridge among identities, offering a public place to bring different groups together around similar interests. (Lord and Blankenship 2016, 222)

These core social functions of museums have been clearly emerging as museum leaders and professionals reflect on how institutions can be relevant and sustainable now and in the future. The Alliance of American Museums 2017 TrendsWatch highlighted empathy and social justice as key forces of change in the field. In a chapter devoted to empathy, report author Elizabeth Merritt states, "[M]useums' inherent strengths position them to be effective 'empathy engines' helping people to understand the 'other' and reinforcing social bonds" (Merritt 2017, 8). To embrace these values of empathy and connection, museums are working to build experiences based in storytelling, lived experience, memory, healing, and civic engagement. Exhibitions are being designed in partnership with community members, content is being co-created between museum staff and visitors, and marginalized voices are being brought into the core of museum spaces.

The International Museum of Folk Art's Gallery of Conscience, inaugurated in 2010, serves as truly unique and visionary example of how museums are experimenting in this area. The gallery's goal is to be an agent of positive social change by engaging history, dialogue, and personal reflection around issues of social justice and human rights. Since the gallery's inception, exhibitions in this space have explored how traditional artists come together in the face of change or disaster to provide comfort, counsel, prayer, and hope through their art. This focus has earned the space membership in the International Coalition of the Sites of Conscience.

Exhibitions in the Gallery of Conscience are "community-driven, co-created, collaborative, participatory, and cumulative," according to a press release. "Visitors and community members become part of the conversation from the very beginning—helping to shape the exhibitions and contribute to the dialogue throughout the exhibition's run." In 2013–2014, the Gallery's exhibition "Let's Talk about This" focused on folk artists' responses to HIV/AIDS through artist and visitor participation, community programs, and a digital storytelling project with LGBTQIA youth developed in partnership with N'MPower and Youth Media Project. The oral histories that were collected were incorporated into the exhibition through listening stations, and also became part of the dialogue-based programs related to the exhibition. Among many other projects, the International Museum of Folk Art is planning an exhibition in 2021–2022 that explores issues of incarceration, prisoners' rights, recidivism, and transitional justice, partnering with Gordon Bernell Charter School, the Santa Fe Youth Detention Center, the Santa Fe Dreamers Project, and the Coalition for Prisoners' Rights, among others.

As museums respond to issues affecting their communities, both locally and globally, there is a clear shift toward focusing on human connection, emotion, and experience as well as the role museums will play as catalysts for human empathy in a society rife with intolerance, discrimination, inequality, social isolation, and self-segregation. In reflecting on their decade-long commitment to dialogue and civic engagement, the leadership team at the Levine Museum of the New South remarked:

> With shared empathy, individuals can move from isolation to belonging, from division to connection, from suspicion to trust, and come together to begin the hard work of creating a cohesive diverse community that values and gives opportunity to all its residents. (Gokcigdem 2016, 235)

STRATEGIES FOR CHANGEMAKERS

So how can we begin to make this shift happen toward a more human-centered mindset? What does this change look like? What is our role as changemakers in advocating for this shift? No matter where you are in your institution, you can take steps toward embracing a human-centered mindset. The rest of this chapter outlines three key strategies for placing people at the core of our museums:

- Building a culture of empathy within our institutions
- Bringing our whole selves to our museum work
- Rethinking institutional hierarchies

1. Building a Culture of Empathy

A key starting place for this type of change is simply practicing more empathy within the workplace environment and culture of a museum institution. While this sounds very broad, it can start with anyone at any level of an organization. In many museums, especially large ones, the proliferation of departments and reporting structures combined with an overreliance on email communication can lead to silos and barriers among staff within the organization. People are not connecting with other people in meaningful ways.

I can speak from my own personal experience, having been in plenty of tense meetings in which everyone comes in with their defenses up, ready to battle. A curator is certain that the education staff are going to "dumb down" their ideas. An educator assumes that their suggestions to make an exhibition more accessible to families will be belittled by an exhibition designer. Situations like these are happening in museums every day, and they are creating or maintaining barriers to change. We're making false assumptions about other people's values and positions without ever listening to their perspectives. However, a culture of empathy can begin to form through the basic building blocks of conversation and listening. Building empathy on an individual level means identifying those people in your organization about whom you might be making assumptions, spending time having a face-to-face conversation with them, taking a step back to truly listen, and trying to gain a greater sense of what they value and why. Being a human-centered museum starts with the human connections and social relationships we build within the institution. Getting this process started can be as easy as having coffee with co-workers you find yourself rarely interacting with or even butting heads with. With the COVID-19 pandemic, we certainly have seen this become even more challenging as staff and volunteers struggle to stay connected through online platforms and video calls. Yet it continues to be important to find new ways to connect with each other, listen, and gain a greater sense of understanding.

In addition to embracing empathy on an individual level, it is vital to consider how museums can embrace a broader form of institutional empathy. Just as individuals can practice listening to and responding to the needs of other individuals, museums have the ability as institutions to mirror those same skills in building empathy with their communities. The work of the Empathetic Museum Group has focused on helping organizations move toward a more empathetic future. According to their model, "an empathetic museum is so connected with its community that it is keenly aware of its values, needs, and challenges" (Empathetic Museum Group 2017b).

Using a rubric called the Maturity Model, museum staff and leaders can assess their own institution's commitment to building empathy across a series of characteristics such as civic vision, institutional body language, community resonance, and sustainability. For museum staff and community members just beginning to think about their work as human-centered, models such as this can provide a spark for meaningful conversations among staff about what it means to be empathetic and better reflect the values of your community. For museums at more advanced stages of this change process, this model can help structure goal setting and inform strategic planning.

So this all sounds great, but what if just a few passionate changemakers are advocating for these ideas and models within an institution? How can these human-centered values of empathy and human connection be integrated into the DNA of an organization, and not just fade if those few passionate staff get frustrated or even leave? Beyond advancing individual empathy as described previously (an important strategy toward spreading empathy within an organization), one key strategy is developing core values and a values statement that reflect these ideas. If your museum does not have any type of core value statement, there is never a bad time to get one drafted. Traditionally, this type of institutional language would be created through a top-down process and likely not have the buy-in of most staff and volunteers. However, it's best to go through a process that allows staff at all levels (even some volunteers and community members) a chance to express their thoughts about a museum's core values. These conversations might even start during hallway conversations or cross-departmental meetings, and trickle up to the leadership team. The goal here is to develop a simple, clear, open, and transparent set of values that can guide everyday decisions and help organizations answer difficult questions and challenges when they arise. If an organization's overall culture does not seem ready for this (yet), a similar process can occur within a single department and then often spread from there. There is always a way to get this process of change happening.

In their essay titled "Adopting Empathy: Why Empathy Should Be a Required Core Value for All Museums—Period," Jon Carfagno and Adam Rozan write about the necessity of integrating empathy throughout an organization's policies and practices, including job descriptions, hiring, and performance review. Through this lens, as they state,

> the leading candidate for a museum's chief curator opening could shift from the person with the strongest publications or acquisitions history to a less experienced curator who had previously worked in the marketing or education departments at another museum because the latter candidate would command a higher qualification in understanding audiences and how to meet their needs. (Carfagno and Rozan 2016, 211)

Having established a set of values based in human connection can more effectively lead to institutions becoming more human-centered and making hiring decisions (like this one) that reflect these values.

The Oakland Museum of California (OMCA) is one institution that has successfully worked to identify, embrace, and implement empathy as a core value and ideology. According to their executive director, Lori Fogarty,

"We have been on a continuous and conscientious journey toward being an empathetic organization for the past ten years" (Empathetic Museum Group 2017a). Through a reinstallation of their collection galleries, a rethink of their programs and exhibitions, and a restructuring of the museum's departments, OMCA has more holistically embraced a connection to topics that influence their visitors and a direct engagement with their local community. While this process has had its challenges, adopting core values of empathy, human connection, and co-creation allows for OMCA to be an agent of change in its community and beyond. "At this point, I believe our staff knows what they're signing up for when they join the Museum," states Fogarty. "Having true employee commitment to this kind of work is essential and that definitely means making some hard decisions" (Empathetic Museum Group 2017a). Chapter 7 explores these ideas further through a conversation with Fogarty about her leadership at OMCA. As we embrace the belief that museums are first and foremost about people, no single museum is incapable of making these same transformations.

2. Bringing Our Whole Selves to Our Work

In addition to practicing more empathy in our work as museum changemakers, it is also important to think consciously about bringing our whole selves to this work. As museum staff, we might too often "clock in" to our jobs and check our own personal passions, values, and identities at the door. The personal communities of our lives float away as we embrace the existing institutional culture and branded identities of our museums. In her book *Presence: Bringing Your Boldest Self to Your Biggest Challenges,* Harvard professor and social psychologist Amy Cuddy discusses her research into personal power in the workplace. "Some organizations," she finds, "socialize new employees by focusing on the groups' identity and needs, failing to acknowledge those of the individuals. Workers may even be discouraged from expressing their true identities" (Cuddy 2015, 54). In most cases, these organizational or group cultures are grounded in legacies of oppression and white, male, patriarchal, colonial values, and they conflict with our personal identities, causing harm. For museums to become truly human-centered and inclusive, we must work toward valuing and celebrating the unique identities, experiences, values, skills, and passions that individuals bring to the institution.

So what does it look like when we bring our whole selves into our work? This core question was asked by Amber Johnson, founder of Justice Fleet, in her powerful opening keynote at the 2017 MuseumNext conference in Portland: "How do we bring our whole selves into our work spaces and what does that look like? What does it mean to say 'This is all of me and I'm going to put all my junk on the table?'" (Johnson 2017). Through her work with Justice Fleet, Johnson is on a mission to start a dialogue about radical inclusion and radical forgiveness, going into neighborhoods to engage their communities in discussions about implicit and explicit bias, social identity, and communicating across difference. Her MuseumNext talk titled "Revolution Requires Forgiveness" focused on the importance of bringing our social identities with us to our professional work, and what it means to allow those identities to truly influence our work. For Johnson, radical inclusion is a deeply personal act that "requires bringing the whole self to the table, [and] the dirty, nasty questions that nobody wants to answer, 'Who am I? What matters to me?'" Beyond this level of deep personal reflection, radical inclusion at the institutional level requires a lot of people within an organization bringing their whole selves to the table. Both radical inclusion and radical forgiveness, as Johnson aptly frames them, are vital to museums becoming more human-centered and ensuring that museums are places that understand, support, and value what every individual brings to this work.

Finally, and perhaps most important, how can museum professionals begin to engage in bringing our whole selves to our work on a daily basis? What are some initial strategies you can adopt right now? In his book *Museums and the Paradox of Change*, scholar and museum activist Robert Janes strongly advocates for museum organizations to connect with the knowledge, experience, and values of individual museum employees and to cultivate personal agency at all levels and departments of an institution. Janes defines personal agency as "the capacity of individual museum workers (not only leaders and managers) to take action in the world" (Janes 2013, 360). He outlines some clear, doable strategies for museum changemakers at all levels (Janes 2013, 347–70):

- Ask yourself, your colleagues, your supervisor, and your leaders "why" you are doing what you are doing. This questioning will help to move the museum beyond the "what" and the "how."
- If there is an intractable issue or situation that is adversely affecting your work, speak out. Advise your manager of the difficulty and ways to address it. Have the courage of your convictions to remedy the situation.
- Decision-making should be decentralized throughout the museum to the "lowest level" in the organization where the work can be done well. In short, staff should have as much responsibility as possible for decisions that affect their work.
- Any person in the museum, irrespective of level or rank, must be free to go directly to any person in the museum for information or assistance needed to perform his or her job.

- When appropriate, share aspects of your nonwork life, whether it be involvement in an environmental nonprofit or work as an artist. These seemingly unrelated skills, knowledge, and experience are essential as a museum broadens its awareness and engages in the interests, issues, and aspirations of its community.

3. Rethinking Hierarchies

To become more human-centered, social organizations that achieve positive impact in their communities, museums need to also rethink their internal organization structures. Most museums rely on deeply ingrained, top-down structures that rely on territorial thinking, defined protocols, and traditional reporting structures based on academic degrees, power, silos, division, and oppression. In these traditional hierarchies, communication flows from the top to the bottom, which means that "innovation stagnates, engagement suffers, and collaboration is virtually non-existent" (Morgan 2015). Furthermore, as stated in the nationwide report *Ready to Lead: Next Generation of Leaders Speak Out*, organizations that maintain traditional hierarchies "risk perpetuating power structures that alienate emerging leadership talent in their organizations" (CompassPoint et al. 2008, 25). The sluggish bureaucracy of this embedded management structure prevents a museum from being responsive to its staff and its broader community. In other words, traditional top-down museums are just not very human-centered. They tend to be leader-centered or focused on a few powerful individuals at the top. Chapter 6 more deeply examines the need for museums to rethink leadership and upend our conventional ways of thinking about authority, power, and hierarchy. So how can this be changed? What steps can we as changemakers take to think about and enact alternative structures?

To be more people-centered, museum leaders and staff can work toward more participatory, democratic, and flatter models for organizational structure. In their book *Creating the Visitor-Centered Museum*, Peter Samis and Mimi Michaelson discuss this transformation that has taken place in museums that take a more visitor-centered approach: "[N]ew ways of working ultimately shift traditional structures and may end up equalizing roles or flattening hierarchies" (Samis and Michaelson 2017, 6). Efforts to decentralize decision-making and promote broader collaboration lead to museums that are more innovative, more responsive to change, and more likely to have a shared central purpose across its staff, volunteers, visitors, and community stakeholders—its human ecosystem. When we rethink and replace the outdated hierarchies, there is clearly a greater potential for a broader base of individuals to feel personal ownership over the meaningful work of museums in their communities.

In 2011, the OCMA made major changes to its structure that resulted in a new cross-disciplinary and cross-functional model focused on visitor experience and community engagement. Referred to within OCMA as "the flower," this new organizational structure attempted to rid the museum of some of the barriers formed by outdated ways of operating. In 2016, the updated organizational chart had "visitor experience & public participation" at its very center, and only text references to the CEO and executive team floating around the outside. What started as a "rake" of institutional silos, according to executive director Lori Fogarty, became a "flower" of cross-functional teams emphasizing transparency, input, and communication. The more decentralized structure has positioned this civic-minded institution to better serve and engage its community, and we have seen that evidenced in the institution's decisions and response after the COVID-19 pandemic.

Aside from reinventing your entire museum's organizational structure (which is awesome, but quite challenging and rare), there are smaller action steps that changemakers can take within their own institution. One way to make these types of changes happen is to work toward flattening communication and expanding participation in decision-making. Seek ideas and input from staff and colleagues on a regular basis. For example, instead of using staff meetings to passively report out information about upcoming exhibitions or new policies, use these times to also discuss critical issues and gather input. Even a large staff meeting can be a platform for two-way communication. In addition, empower staff at all levels to participate in setting goals for their departments and for the museum. While this may take a greater investment in time, it will lead to broader feelings of ownership once those goals are being implemented and achieved on the floor with visitors. Involving staff at all levels of an organization in goal-setting and decision-making can also work toward cultivating leadership at all levels. Human-centered museums are institutions that recognize leaders across all levels and departments, not just at the top.

Finally, one important strategy for embracing a human-centered mindset in museums involves replacing outdated "org charts" with new ways of visualizing connections. Everyone reading this is probably familiar with the org charts that have each position in a box, and lines that connect everyone based on management and reporting. Who manages who? Who evaluates who? Who has power over who? These charts fan out from the director or CEO box at the top, ending at the bottom with lots of little boxes filled with part-time staff, security guards, volunteer docents, and so on. Not only are these charts confusing (and often quite ugly), but they emphasize oppressive power relationships and do not accurately represent the way a museum works and how staff interact with each other.

We need to replace these old org charts with new maps that emphasize human connection and collaboration. And you don't need to be the human resources director or CEO to give this a try. Draw a circle to represent yourself, and then begin adding in other staff based on your working relationships with them. Who do you collaborate with on a regular basis? What working group meetings or committee meetings do you attend? What are some of the social connections you have within your organization? (Yes, these count, too.) Soon, you begin creating an organic map of your organization based on human relationships and connection. Not only is this a great way to visualize and map your existing connections with others, but you can also use this as a way to identify individuals or departments in your organization that you are currently not connected with. What are some ways you might begin to develop new connections to those people? What effect might building new connections have on your work, their work, and the museum's work in the broader community?

In her widely watched TED Talk titled "The Power of Vulnerability," researcher and author Brené Brown talks about connection as a fundamental human experience. "Connection is why we're here," she says. "It's what gives purpose and meaning to our lives" (Brown 2010). During a time when we are surrounded by an increasingly fragmented society of "us versus them," museums have the potential to be powerful catalysts for empathy and human connection. As changemakers, we need to truly embrace, value, and celebrate the people who make up museums—its staff and volunteers as well as members, donors, visitors, neighbors, community partners, and the broader public. These people, more than anything else, give museums their meaning and purpose, and it is the people that form the basis for any process of making change happen.

REFERENCES

Bahr-Reisinger, Gesine. 2016. "How Museums Can Help to Save the World: A Conversation with Stefan Weber, the Director of the Museum für Islamische Kunst." Stiftung Preussischer Kulturbesitz. https://www.preussischer-kulturbesitz.de/en/newsroom/dossiers-and-news/all-dossiers/dossier-heimat-home/how-museums-can-help-to-save-the-world.html.
Bautista, Susana Smith. 2014. *Museums in the Digital Age*. London: Routledge.
Brown, Brené. 2010. "The Power of Vulnerability." Filmed June 2010 in Houston, TX. TED video. https://www.ted.com/talks/brene_brown_the_power_of_vulnerability/transcript.
Carfagno, Jon, and Adam Rozan. 2016. "Adopting Empathy: Why Empathy Should Be a Required Core Value for All Museums—Period." In *Fostering Empathy through Museums*, edited by Elif M. Gokcigdem. Lanham, MD: Rowman & Littlefield.
CompassPoint Nonprofit Services, The Eugene and Agnes E. Meyer Foundation, and the Annie E. Casey Foundation. 2008. *Ready to Lead? Next Generation Leaders*

Speak Out. https://www.compasspoint.org/sites/default/files/documents/521_ready tolead2008.pdf.

Cuddy, Amy. 2015. *Presence: Bringing Your Boldest Self to Your Biggest Challenges.* New York: Little, Brown and Company.

Cutler, Anna. 2013. "Who Will Sing the Song? Learning Beyond Institutional Critique." Tate Papers, no. 19. https://www.tate.org.uk/research/publications/tate -papers/19/who-will-sing-the-song-learning-beyond-institutional-critique.

Delaney, Brigid. 2016. "Philosopher Roman Krznaric: 'We Are in More Urgent Need of Empathy Than Ever Before.'" *The Guardian.* https://www.theguardian.com/ books/2016/feb/19/empathy-expert-roman-krznaric-on-shifting-away-from-20th -century-individualism.

Dewey, John. (1934) 2005. *Art as Experience.* Reprint, New York: Perigree. Citations refer to the Perigree edition.

Empathetic Museum Group. 2017a. "Honor Roll: The Oakland Museum of California." http://empatheticmuseum.weebly.com/honor-roll—blog/archives/05-2017.

———. 2017b. "Maturity Model Rubric." http://empatheticmuseum.weebly.com/ maturity-model.html.

Gokcigdem, Elif M. 2016. *Fostering Empathy through Museums.* Lanham, MD: Rowman & Littlefield.

Janes, Robert. 2013. *Museums and the Paradox of Change.* London: Routledge.

Johnson, Amber. 2017. "Revolution Requires Forgiveness." Presented at MuseumNext, Portland, OR.

Krznaric, Roman. 2013. "How to Start an Empathy Revolution." Filmed June 2010 in Athens, Greece. TED video. https://www.youtube.com/watch?v=RT5X6NIJR88.

———. 2014. *Empathy: Why It Matters, and How to Get It.* New York: Penguin.

———. 2015. "At the World's First Empathy Museum, Visitors Walk a Mile in Another Person's Shoes—Literally." *YES Magazine*, August 22, 2015. https:// www.yesmagazine.org/health-happiness/2015/08/22/at-the-worlds-first-empathy -museum-visitors-walk-a-mile-in-another-persons-shoes-literally/.

Lord, Gail Dexter, and Ngaire Blankenship. 2016. *Cities, Museums, and Soft Power.* Washington, DC: AAM Press.

Merritt, Elizabeth. 2017. *Alliance of American Museums 2017 TrendsWatch.* https:// www.aam-us.org/programs/center-for-the-future-of-museums/trendswatch-2017/.

Morgan, Jacob. 2015. "The 5 Types of Organizational Structures: Part 1, The Hierarchy." *Forbes*, July 6, 2015. https://www.forbes.com/sites/jacobmorgan/2015/07/06/ the-5-types-of-organizational-structures-part-1-the-hierarchy.

Notter, Jamie, and Maddie Grant. 2011. *Humanize: How People-Centric Organizations Succeed in a Social World.* Indianapolis: Que.

Rainie, Lee, and Barry Wellman. 2012. *Networked: The New Social Operating System.* Cambridge, MA: MIT Press.

Samis, Peter, and Mimi Michaelson. 2017. *Creating the Visitor-Centered Museum.* London: Routledge.

Visser, Jasper. 2013. "From Social Media to a Social Museum." The Nordic Centre of Heritage Learning. http://nckultur.org/wp-content/uploads/2013/06/From_So cial_Media_to_a_Social_Museum_Jasper_Visser.pdf.

2

Let Your Community In

During the summer of 2017, I made my first visit to the Santa Cruz Museum of Art and History (MAH)—a pilgrimage of sorts to this institution led, at the time, by author and change agent Nina Simon. She had invited me to be a "camp counselor" for their summer MuseumCamp, and I could not turn down a chance to visit the MAH, see what makes it tick, and be a part of this community of changemakers. Not only have I been a longtime reader of the *Museum 2.0* blog and a huge fan of Nina's books on museums, but the MAH had just officially opened Abbott Square, an adjacent public plaza that the museum converted to a bustling community gathering place and food market. For me, the Santa Cruz museum and Nina's leadership has been one of the exemplars in turning an institution toward a focus on its local community. In addition, Nina and several members of her team at the MAH have been inspirational changemakers for so many across the museum field. After arriving as executive director at the MAH in 2011, Nina worked with her team to tirelessly transform the MAH into a thriving museum and community center for Santa Cruz.

It's one thing for a museum to talk the talk when it comes to community engagement, and entirely another thing to walk the walk and make change happen. After spending several days at the MAH, going on a "running meeting" with Nina at a nearby state park, and meeting staff that develop programs and exhibitions, I knew that they meant business and were truly dedicated to making the museum a place at the core of their community, and bringing community into the core of their institution. I was fortunate to visit during their exhibition *Lost Childhoods*, an issue-driven exhibition that the MAH staff created with their community. Showcasing the stories, struggles, and triumphs of youth who are aging out of foster care, this powerful exhibition was co-created with the Foster Youth Museum and a group of over one hundred local foster youth, artists, and youth advocates. This community was at the core of the exhibition, and there was even a large wall text that boldly declared, "We made this with our community." Through years of getting to know its local community and becoming intertwined with its people, the MAH team has embodied a shift from being a museum "for" its community to being a museum "of" and "by" its community. And it has continued to do so in exhibitions, programs, and community-based partnerships ever since.

Being at the MAH for MuseumCamp was just icing on the cake. Starting in 2013, the MAH hosted MuseumCamp as a professional development experience that is part retreat, part unconference, and part adult summer camp at the museum. It always brought together a wide range of artists and creative professionals working in diverse contexts and communities. Amid all the workshops, small-group discussions, beach trips, and conversations with over a hundred passionate changemakers, one moment back in 2017 resonated with me more than any other—perhaps because of how simple and straightforward it was. Portland-based writer, game critic, and creative entrepreneur Josh Boykin stepped up to the microphone during a series of fast-paced lightning talks. Josh works outside museums, yet cares a great deal about building community. Although he lives and works in Portland, Oregon, our paths had not yet crossed. His lightning talk was personal and inspiring, yet there's one simple thing about his talk that has stuck in my mind. Projected on the screen behind him during the entire duration of his talk were four words, large and bold: "Let Your Community In."

Since that moment, Josh's message has become one of my mantras when it comes to being a museum changemaker. How do museums make the shift to "let community in"? Is community always separate from and outside museums, in need of being "let in"? What does *community* even mean? Like many museum educators, I have grappled with these questions my entire career, yet the complexities and challenges of engaging communities came into focus through some of my more recent work in community partnerships.

This chapter will guide you through the essential process of defining the concept of *community* with your work as a changemaker, identifying ways to break down the barriers between museums and their communities as well as build relevance through local community partnerships. It's so important for museums to be a local place intertwined with and inseparable from local realities and issues. Museums are located in our communities, but they're also a part of those communities. How do we as changemakers within museums work to define our place, our town, our city, our neighborhood, and our community, and how do we learn about the people in our place, what connects us, and what brings people together into a community?

A MEANINGLESS WORD?

The term *community* may very well be one of the most frequently used words these days when it comes to describing the shifting goals, values, programs, exhibitions, staff and audience demographics, and even communication strategies of museums. In fact, I've already used this word more than thirty times in just the opening few pages of this chapter. For decades, museums (and most funding organizations, too) have been increasingly using phrases like "aiming to serve our community," "reaching out to our communities," and "strengthening our community" to create a sense of a museum's broader mission and social purpose. In describing its Museums Empowered funding initiative, the Institute of Museum and Library Services (IMLS) states that "museums are at the forefront of change in our communities" and they serve as "strong community anchors" (Institute of Museum and Library Services [IMLS] 2018a). In their thirteen-page strategic plan for 2018–2022 titled *Transforming Communities*, the word *community* or *communities* is used thirty-six times (IMLS 2018a).

Museums and cultural organizations are constantly being asked how effectively they are serving their communities and how well they represent their community. But foundations, granting organizations, civic entities, and funders do not have a consistent definition of what they even mean by *community*. We can begin to read between the lines when we are asked about the zip codes we serve, the number of Title I schools visiting, and what programs we have for "at-risk" youth or "underserved" audiences. The best sense I can get from how IMLS defines community or communities is "people of diverse geographic, cultural, and socioeconomic backgrounds" or "families and individuals of diverse cultural and socioeconomic backgrounds and needs." Whether we are defining these groups based on geography, interests, or experience, are we essentially talking about people who are not engaging with our institutions?

Nina Simon writes about the common misuse of the word *community* to refer to the general public or "everyone who doesn't currently visit here" (Simon 2009). Museum expert Porchia Moore discusses the dangers of using the word *community* in a reductive way, such as when it is used to describe a large group of people by focusing on a single attribute. In the context of discussions about inclusion, Moore writes, "'Community' becomes code for discussing black and brown visitors" (Moore 2015). Referring to a group as "the black community" or "the LGBTQ community" can be extremely problematic when groups are perceived as a monolithic or singular community. Moore advocates for museums to dig deeper into this language and how it reflects the decisions we make to develop one-off programs or exhibitions. Overall, there is a generally agreed-upon sense that reaching out to and engaging with community is a good thing for museums. Yet how do we effectively do this work and advocate for it if we don't truly have a sense of what it means beyond connecting with "those other people" out there?

As museums vaguely define *community* or *communities* as groups that might not be engaging or connecting with the museum, there is also a troubling binary and divide we have created between "museum" and "community." It's so ingrained in the way so many of us talk about museum practice, myself included. We have been trained to think of museums as separate from communities; they are seen as buildings with collections, objects, exhibitions, and experts that are made available to communities on a limited basis. Referring to some functions of the museum as "outreach" just reinforces this separation. By default, museums then exist as disconnected, disengaged, and distanced from this idea of community. We might be feeding this gap by simply not addressing it.

So in many ways, the word *community* has become a vague and almost meaningless expression. Museum professionals use it too frequently and in ways that overlook the inherent complexities. I fully realize that by writing this chapter, I'm engaging in overuse of the term myself, but my interest here lies in unpacking the term and opening up many of the rich complexities tied up in this concept. Rather than stop using this word or replace it with something else, I'm advocating for those working for and with museums to gain a deeper understanding of what *community* means. I believe it is a meaningful concept, and I am thoroughly excited to see it being used more frequently by museums and funding organizations. We just need to explore and address the complexities involved with defining *community* and *communities* for our institutions. Through this chapter, I offer up a set of principles and strategies useful for museum changemakers to clearly define what *community* means to them in support of meaningfully expanding this work. Yet this is just a starting point. Each institution has to create its own definition of community and work to bring in local expertise, knowledge, and lived experiences as it works to expand this practice within the institution.

DEFINING *COMMUNITY*

Obviously, there is no single definition for the word *community*. And it does not benefit this conversation to check with Webster's dictionary, because the traditional definition of community is vague and outdated. In his influential book *Community: The Structure of Belonging*, Peter Block offers an exploration of community building and the ways that healthy, restorative communities emerge and sustain themselves. Defining community as "the experience of belonging," Block writes, "We are in a community each time we find a place where we belong" (Block 2008, xii). Author and curator Gaynor Kavanagh defines *community* as "the sense of belonging that comes to those who are part of it" (Kavanagh 1990, 68). This core sense of belonging has two meanings. It is about having a sense of relatedness and being a part of something, and it is about having a sense of ownership and acting as a creator or co-owner of that community. For Fabian Pfortmüller, an entrepreneur and author who studies community building across the globe, community is "a group of people that care about each other and feel they belong together" (Pfortmüller 2017).

First and foremost, then, community is about people. At its core is a set of human relationships, not just a place, organization, idea, or internet platform. Second, it is important to recognize that people participate in and identify with multiple communities at the same time. We might belong to a church, feel affinity to people in our neighborhood, be connected with those at our school, and bond with others who share an aspect of our personal identity (age, sexuality, ethnicity, language, etc.)—all on the same day. We all belong to many communities, some that we define for ourselves and some that are defined for us. Our participation in certain communities might be deep, long-term, and really meaningful to us, while our involvement in other communities might be fairly thin and insignificant. It's also important to note that the social relationships that form communities are fluid, constantly shifting given time and changing circumstances. While it seems obvious that formal institutions (schools, churches, museums, and nonprofits) play an important role in forming communities, we also need to recognize the powerful role of informal institutions (the neighborhood barbershop, a local grocery co-op, a community choir group, or a gardening club). Through each of these communities, we might come together to feel various degrees of shared belonging, trust, mutual interests, and safety.

On top of these ways to define *community*, I want to layer on the transformative belief in a "beloved community" that comes from the teachings of Martin Luther King Jr., as well as more recent writings by Grace Lee Boggs and bell hooks. It is the idea of community as an agent of change, engaged in the struggle for justice and the well-being of the whole. In her book *Killing Rage: Ending Racism*, hooks writes:

> Beloved community is formed not by the eradication of difference but by its affirmation, by each of us claiming the identities and cultural legacies that shape who we are and how we live in the world. (hooks 1996, 265)

This affirmative vision of community is based, in part, on finding common ground through social justice and the possibility of radical change as well as the transformative element of shared responsibility. Community is not merely a passive gathering of people around shared interests or shared geography, but rather the form through which these shared understandings take on life as collective action. As hooks states, "the commitment to community is what gives us the inspiration to come up with ways to resolve conflict" (Brosi and hooks 2012, 76).

This more active notion of community, or building community, also connects deeply to the concept of "bridging" popularized by Robert Putnam, author of *Bowling Alone: The Collapse and Revival of American Community* (2000). In this groundbreaking book, Putnam examined the disconnection pervasive across our society. He explored how we might begin to strengthen a sense of connection through social networks and building social capital, a value that forms from trust, reciprocity, and cooperation associated with social networks. One form of social capital is created through "bonding" among homogenous, exclusive, inward-facing groups. Another, more powerful, form of social capital is created through "bridging" diverse, heterogeneous, inclusive, and outward-looking groups through activities of sharing, exchange, and consensus building.

The *Better Together* report, published by the Saguaro Seminar in 2000, took a look at the role of the arts and museums in successfully building social capital in the United States. The report argues that arts and culture organizations can nurture connectedness and bridging by "strengthening friendships, helping communities to understand and celebrate their heritage, and providing safe ways to discuss and solve difficult social problems" (Crooke 2007, 68). Overall, the report recommended key principles to guide the arts, including encouragement of initiatives that form bridges across race, income, gender, religion, and generations as well as including arts and culture in community planning and organizing. While this report is certainly not new, these principles continue to be valuable as we reflect on the work of museums.

The concepts of beloved community and the social capital of bridging both celebrate difference, and work toward bringing people together to form and strengthen new relationships. Overlap these defining characteristics of community with the ideas of a human-centered museum that I explore in chapter 1, and we find deep commonalities of human connection, social relationships, and a commitment to change. For me, these overarching ideas form the basis for any productive discussion of community and how we then work as changemakers to build an institution's connection within its community. As Elizabeth Crooke writes in her book *Museums and Community*:

> To be of value, museums need to find significance within these communities—without those connections, the museum and its collections will be of little importance. It is people who bring the value and consequence to objects and

collections; as a result, if a museum cannot forge associations with people, it will have no meaning. (Crooke 2007, 131)

COMMUNITY AS THE HEART OF AN INSTITUTION

It's so important for museums to be a local place intertwined with inseparable from the local realities and issues. For many museums, so much of this idea of community is grounded in geography: how we define our place, our town, our city, our neighborhood, and how we learn about the people in this place, what connects us, and what brings us together into a community. Our institutions can become more grounded in our local communities when we open our ears and our hearts to let others get involved in new and different ways. As museums engage more deeply with local residents both within their own buildings and out in community spaces, the more interconnectedness that exists between those museums and their local communities. Cultivating relationships among museums and local communities opens up the potential to bring about positive change in residents' lives and making museums more accountable and responsive to local residents. And this has never felt more urgent than after the COVID-19 pandemic dramatically changed who visits museums, and how close they live to the institutions they feel comfortable and safe visiting in light of COVID-19-related health guidelines and recommendations. This reliance on local visitors and audiences is likely to have a shift in museums that we can't yet see or understand as I write these pages. And while the pandemic may be forcing museums to connect with local audiences and neighborhoods, some institutions have been doing this work for years, including the Queens Museum in New York.

Beginning in 2006 with the hiring of their first community organizer, Naila Caicedo-Rosario, the Queens Museum began a journey toward becoming more connected with and responsive to its local neighborhood and community. Through their Heart of Corona initiative and other projects that have emerged in the past decade—like the Immigrant Movement International, the New New Yorkers program, and Studio in the Park, to name just a few—the team at the Queens Museum has been actively working beyond the walls of the museum to build close ties with its diverse local neighborhood. Key projects have meaningfully involved local residents in envisioning and leading programs that address a wide range of issues relevant to the largely immigrant community, from health care and housing to immigrant rights and neighborhood identity. As community organizer Naila Caicedo-Rosario powerfully states, "The museum sees the community as not just potential audience members but as the real heart of the institution" (Mogilevich et al. 2016, 22).

A large part of their work has focused on a single neighborhood adjacent to the museum—Corona, defined as one of the most diverse, vibrant, dense, fast-growing, and predominantly immigrant neighborhoods in New York City. Over the course of a few years, museum staff had regular conversations with community leaders, social service organizations, community board representatives, organizations representing immigrant communities, local media, activists, and elected officials. They listened to the experiences and needs of local residents and began deepening communication and trust between community members and the museum. "You can't come in, 'say this is a crisis' and expect communities that have been doing work on the ground to immediately trust you," says Prerana Reddy, who served as director of public events for the Queens Museum and played a pivotal role in these community conversations and planning processes. "These relationships have to be built over time. You have to commit to be part of the movement and offer the resources you have, beyond just art or artists, to immigrant-led organizations" (Rajagopalan 2017). Museum staff and community leaders mapped out the cultural assets of the neighborhood, not just its challenges. Throughout the Corona Plaza and Heart of Corona initiatives, the Queens Museum clearly identified its core challenge: how can we substantively engage the many immigrant communities that live in Corona in co-creating a dignified public space for the neighborhood we share? (Mogilevich et al. 2016).

The Corona Plaza project has since become a thriving community development initiative in the neighborhood. The plaza has been reimagined, and now serves as an open public space for connection, cultural celebrations, and active local involvement as well as a central site for the Queens Museum's public art programs and festivals. Silvia Juliana Mantilla Ortiz, Corona community organizer and artist services coordinator at the Queens Museum, remarked:

> Folks are imagining and creating within our communities all the time, but they're not usually framed as art or creative cultural practices. I think opening up spaces where that creativity can be engaged and named and uplifted and made more public is a big part of what Corona Plaza is about. That's the way folks build community, through culture. Corona Plaza acts as a platform where folks can connect and make visible the things that are already happening. (Mogilevich et al. 2016, 39)

One longtime partner of the Queens Museum has been Mujeres en Movimiento (MEM), a Corona-based collective with over 150 members, mostly immigrant Latina women. This group's main goal is to build community empowerment through exercise by practicing dance therapy, fitness workshops, and bicycling in their neighborhood. The Queens Museum worked with

MEM members to create an exhibit of immigrant rights art at the museum as well as a series of walking tours, performances, and bicycle routes. "The work of Mujeres en Movimiento to empower their neighbors and networks through information is precisely the type of inspiring community action that the City wants to uplift and support at this important moment for so many of our residents," stated Nisha Agarwal, New York City's Immigrant Affairs commissioner (Trouillot 2017).

In 2017, the Reinvestment Fund and IMLS published a report titled *Strengthening Networks, Sparking Change* that largely discusses the role of museums and libraries as catalysts for social well-being, collective influence, and positive change in their local communities. In this report, the authors bring attention to the community-engagement model of the Queens Museum, writing:

> By making a commitment to a particular neighborhood and deploying an adaptable community-organizing approach, the Queens Museum has built strong relationships with local entities and a sterling reputation among near neighbors. The combination of relationship-building and a willingness to take on new issues has enabled the museum to be more strategic in the work it takes on, and therefore increased the likelihood that its activities will have significant and sustained impact. (IMLS 2017, 49).

VALUING COMMUNITY

This may sound radical, but I believe it's also a fact: our community knows more than we do. There is so much expertise and knowledge outside our institutions that we tend to reject and ignore, but it's greater than what we hold on to within our institutions. We have got to start breaking down these walls, listen more, and rethink the way we value some knowledge and stories over others. As changemakers, we need to recognize and value the assets of our communities—their stories, experiences, creative energies, and knowledges. What if we could effectively recenter this movement for change in museums around our local communities and the power, knowledge, creativity, and capacities that they can bring to our institutions? The Queens Museum is not only a great example of how a museum clearly defines community and works closely to partner with a local neighborhood, but it also indicates how important it is for institutions to value community experience, cultural practices, stories, and knowledge.

When museums begin to develop relationships with certain communities, they must understand the power dynamics involved. Most museums hold a great deal of institutional power and authority, so many relationships or partnerships with community groups begin in a situation of imbalance and inequity. It is important to recognize that museums are understood "to represent those who have privileges in society, i.e., the educated, the relatively wealthy, those who are in control through either their status . . . or through direct political power" (Watson 2007, 10). This power extends to a museum's architecture, collections and collecting practices, exhibitions, scholarship, and interpretation. It is also important to recognize the tension in most museums between traditional academic scholarship and community input. Consulting with community knowledge holders can often be viewed as an erosion of scholarship and curatorial confidence, and working with community-based artists can be seen as lowering accepted standards of "quality." On top of all of this baggage, the Western, white, colonial concept of museums may not necessarily be relevant or valued in many communities who have been excluded or oppressed by this system.

For community relationships to grow and thrive, museums need to step back in their role as authorities and see community members as experts on their own needs and local assets. Identifying community assets and valuing resident participation works to empower residents and legitimize these community partnerships. Stacey Marie Garcia, who served as the director of community engagement at the Santa Cruz MAH for many years, has both researched and enacted community and civic engagement practices, methods, and theories in museums. In her eyes, "it's not solely about how museums can serve communities but rather what are the communities' resources, knowledge and interests that can inform museum practice? Furthermore, how can museums and communities work together to share strengths in the community?" (Garcia 2012b).

At the core of our work with specific communities and local neighborhoods is the practice of identifying and embracing the strengths, creative skills, stories, languages, cultures, voices, and experiences that come from our communities. In the overall research on community development, this is referred to as an *asset-based* approach or *capacity-focused* development. This thinking runs counter to the mindset of a *needs-based* approach that focuses too much on problems and deficiencies in a community or neighborhood, and thus how institutions can "serve their needs." "This phrase drives me nuts," writes Nina Simon. "It smacks of paternalism. As if it weren't enough to be experts on our subject matter. Now we're the experts on what people 'need' too?" (Simon 2016, 92). Rather than telling communities what they need and how they should do things differently, museums can instead center the gifts and creative capacities of communities as we work toward building relationships based in trust and mutual respect.

According to foundational work in the field of asset-based community development, this approach focuses on identifying community assets and strengths, and is both community driven and relationship driven. Rather than asking, "What are the needs of your community?" we can approach these conversations from a asset-based and community-driven approach. Key questions might instead be: What do you value most about your community? When was a time you felt your community was at its best? What is the essence of your community that makes it unique and strong?

Finally, thinking about community development work through an asset-based approach tends to build relationships among community members. As Graeme Stuart, community development specialist and activist, writes:

> The real value in asset mapping is bringing people together so they can discover each other's strengths and resources, and to think about how they can build on what is already in the community. One way we can do this is by fostering the relationships, or the place, where assets can be productive and powerful together. (Stuart 2018)

Museums and cultural organizations hold the potential to be these places where community assets can be powerful together. As changemakers, we just need to take bold steps to value the skills, interests, culture, and heritage of our communities and neighborhoods and begin to decenter the traditional power structures of museum institutions. For museums truly invested in valuing and working with local residents or groups, we must step back and bring these community members into roles that make decisions, shape policies, and change practices that directly affect impacted communities. And as uncomfortable and messy as this might be for so many museums, we have got to start somewhere and make this change happen.

A PROFOUND EXPERIMENT: *PHILADELPHIA ASSEMBLED*

In 2017, the Philadelphia Museum of Art stepped way outside its comfort zone to host the most community-collaborative project in its over 140-year history. The project was sparked by Dutch artist, curator, and activist Jeanne van Heeswijk, and began with conversations she had with people and community organizations across the city of Philadelphia. Through her socially engaged art practice, van Heeswijk seeks to engage citizens in the enactment of social change within their own communities. After nearly four years of community-centered planning, the museum presented "Philadelphia Assembled," a massive collaboration with 150 artists, activists, construction workers, residents, and community organizations in an attempt to connect the museum to the neighborhoods and issues facing Philadelphia in the contemporary world.

The first public phase of the project launched in spring of 2017 as a series of more than sixty public events and art installations outside the museum walls. There were community garden art installations, pop-up plays, community marches, a bus that traveled around the city to engage residents in discussions about economic justice and environmental racism, community meals, and a gathering space at the city's African Cultural Art Forum for conversations about land and economic sovereignty. "For the Philadelphia Art Museum to take on this huge project and go out into communities and to begin to foster real relationships gives me hope. It feels bigger than art," remarked artist Staci Moore, member of the Women's Community Revitalization Project and whose work was featured in the exhibition (Terruso 2017).

The entire project culminated later in 2017 with a participatory exhibition in the museum's Perelman Building that reassembled and reunited works and ideas that emerged from the previous public actions. A decentralized network of local artists and community activists developed the exhibition with museum staff from across departments. Visitors to the galleries experienced a large wall-sized map of Pennsylvania showing the locations of prisons and portraits of inmates, an extensive timeline of migration and colonialism, an exhibit on Black-owned businesses, a six-by-six-foot quilt that displays seventy years of life in the Kensington neighborhood, two geodesic domes created as sanctuary spaces, and much more.

"This is the museum engaged in community work at its finest, or at its most extreme," said Damon Reaves, who served as associate curator of Community, Engagement, and Access at the museum during this project (Salisbury 2017). For a large institution grounded in so much tradition and history, it was quite a leap of faith to work so fully with its local communities for more than four years. The project challenged museum staff in many ways, forcing the museum to give up some of its control and hand over some of its authority to local activists, small nonprofits, and artists. Local residents and community members were asked to connect with this behemoth of an art museum, an institution many had felt excluded from; some left with a sense of hope for the future.

Whether this hope is realized is up to the team at the Philadelphia Museum of Art and their efforts to keep these community relationships alive. While there were certainly mistakes, missteps, and challenges throughout this project, it represents a meaningful experiment for one of the country's largest public art museums. "For us, as an institution, it's been life-changing and profound," continues Reaves. "We're humbled to participate in this kind of conversation and grateful the collaborators allowed us to participate. We want to be part of that civil dialogue" (Crimmins 2017).

STRATEGIES FOR CHANGEMAKERS

So how can we begin to make this shift happen and bring community into the core of our practice? What does this change look like? No matter where you are in your practice, you can take steps toward breaking down barriers between museums and communities. As Nina Simon writes, "Connecting with communities means making conscious decisions that invite in particular people. It means making some conscious choices that push your institution towards being more of a 'third space'" (Simon 2009). The rest of this chapter outlines three key strategies for adopting more community-centered practice in museums and making this change happen:

- Define community for yourself.
- Develop community advisory groups.
- Create partnerships.

1. Define Community for Yourself

Define what you mean by *community* and whom you are targeting when you engage in community outreach and partnerships. This can begin by having small, open conversations at your institution about how individuals define community. Start with those you work with closely, and then have coffee with five individuals you don't work with regularly. Ask what *community* means to them. What communities do they feel a part of? What communities is your museum connecting with, and what communities do they think you are not connecting with? No matter where you are in your organization, work toward bringing these discussions to senior management and leadership.

These conversations can often begin with geography and place. Where are you located, and to what extent are you focusing on your specifically local community? This can be as simple as your immediate neighborhood, town, city, or county. Many times, museums have such a broad sense of their audience and "the public" that they completely ignore those residents living around them. How many people living adjacent to your museum would consider your organization to be a part of the neighborhood? Using geographic locations to help define community can also bring together people with a diverse range of backgrounds, interests, experiences, and creative assets, which lends itself to building social capital of the "bridging" kind.

In her book *Museums Involving Communities*, Margaret Kadoyama discusses a series of questions and key steps to determining "priority communities." Museum leadership should be clear about identifying the priority communities that they want to connect with more fully, and why they are interested in those specific communities. For Kadoyama, it is also important to recognize that "'community' is not the same as 'audience'" (Kadoyama 2018, 93). It is quite valuable to this process to be specific about defining your community and then going about a thorough process of learning about those communities (demographic research, surveys, interviews, focus groups, etc.).

Nina Simon provides a few simple questions to ask ourselves when we begin this process (Simon 2015):

- Can you define the community to whom you want to be relevant?
- Can you describe them?
- What do they care about?
- What is useful to them?
- What is on their minds?

Remember to keep a focus on community assets and refrain from getting stuck thinking about the deficits and deficiencies of a particular community or neighborhood. Explore the range of asset-mapping tools that already exist, and discover a process that works best for you, your institution, and your set of core values.

2. Develop Community Advisory Groups

Perhaps one of the most important elements of driving community-centered practices in any organization is listening to and involving community voices when shaping this process. One initial way to do this is to form community advisory groups. These groups can be temporary and project-focused or permanent and long-lasting. They can be created with leaders and representatives from one single community or neighborhood, or they can represent a wide range of communities with which your museum is working to connect. The goal is to find the right fit with your organization, its size, its organizational culture, and your goals for becoming a museum of, by, and for its community. For some museums, a large formal advisory committee is going to function best, and for other museums it might be best to plan a monthly potluck meal with local residents.

As you form your own community advisory group or groups, it is good to go into the process with some key questions to define who should be part of the group and why. Through their Heart of Corona initiative, staff from the Queens Museum used a range of meaningful questions, including:

- What are the different voices in your neighborhood?
- Who are the community-based organizations who have been doing work in the neighborhood for a long time? How can you start listening to them now?
- How can your organization be flexible and learn to work with organizations and people who have different ways of doing things than you do?

In her discussion of advisory groups, Kadoyama brings some clear, important guidance for anyone exploring this process. "It is critical to understand the importance of *valuing the diverse perspectives* that advisory committee members bring," she writes, "and for one's organizations to *demonstrate a commitment to follow through*" (Kadoyama 2018, 116).

Before you get started, be sure to ask yourself: does my institution really want our community to shape this? If your museum's leadership doesn't want to hear what your community members have to say and if your organization is not ready to take action in response to their input and guidance, then perhaps you're not ready for a community advisory group. You just simply might have more work to do in shifting your organization to value community perspectives before you begin to invite those perspectives in.

In my experience developing and working with advisory groups, I have learned how important it is to be very clear up front about the purpose of the group. Define what is expected of community members, what your museum's commitment is to this process, and what outcomes might be expected. Always be transparent with your community advisors, and keep open and clear communication with them. You are building relationships of trust and mutual support, and being honest will help build these relationships.

As you set out to develop your own community advisory groups, do some homework and find out what other museums and institutions (locally or outside your area) have successfully developed these processes. You might even want to create a short profile document of other museums doing this work, which can be useful at meetings with other staff who might not trust this process or understand its value. I wanted to list a few here, which I see as exemplars in this work and worth learning more about.

Wing Luke Museum of the Asian Pacific American Experience

In 2006, the Wing Luke developed their Community Advisory Committee, a group of core community members who serve as primary decision-makers for exhibition development, creating content, and guiding evaluation. Each exhibition has its own committee, and the museum strives to ensure that staff do not overpower the conversation, but rather listen and are responsive to the

ideas and concerns of committee members (Garcia 2012a, 13–14). The museum has been focused on influencing their community for more than twenty
years, and their dedication to the community process has led to national and
international recognition.

Children's Creativity Museum in San Francisco

Formed in 2011, the Creative Community Council was a group of youth
and adult advocates who were tasked with a specific action of creating a
platform for outreach and engagement. They closely examined the demographics of San Francisco, identified specific neighborhoods in order to target
underserved youth and families, and wrapped up their work by developing a
strategic Community Outreach and Engagement Plan for the museum.

Santa Cruz Museum of Art and History

In 2012, the MAH launched its Creative Community Committee, a diverse
group of multigenerational community representatives from social services, the
arts, business, education, the city, technology, and their board of directors. The
group meets bimonthly to help museum staff understand and brainstorm ways
the museum can collaboratively address the needs and assets of a vast array of
communities in Santa Cruz County. The cohorts of this groups have been central
to planning and implementing community-centered exhibitions at the MAH.

Portland Art Museum

In 2016, the Portland Art Museum formed its Native Art Advisory Group
under the leadership of then-curator of Native American Art Deana Dartt.
This group of representatives and artists from Native communities was pivotal in guiding and supporting the museum's Center for Contemporary Native
Arts, which opened in 2015 and served as a core part of the museum's efforts
to center Native perspectives, expand its presentation of contemporary Native
artists and voices, and increase Native participation through programs, audience development, and exhibition planning.

Phillips Collection

Before opening their community-based art center, the Town Hall Education
Arts Recreation Campus, in 2018, the museum conducted an eight-month
community advisory committee. This group of staff and community stakeholders worked together to determine needs, assets, goals, and programmatic

directions in collaboration with Ward 7 and 8 community organizations and the East of the River community.

Studio Museum in Harlem

As part of their major building project scheduled to be completed in 2021 and the inHarlem initiative, the Studio Museum created their Community Advisory Network, a group of Harlem residents, teachers, parents, and community representatives working to deepen the museum's roots in their neighborhood and preserve Harlem's cultural heritage and oral histories.

3. Create Partnerships

As museum staff work more closely with community organizations, stakeholders, and leaders, it can be mutually beneficial to develop more long-term and structured partnerships. Unfortunately, the word *partnership* can be thrown around a lot in the work of museums. What museums frequently call *community partnerships* tend to be short-term, one-off relationships that primarily focus on benefiting a museum's programming or exhibitions.

Effective community partnerships, however, are rooted in trust, develop over time, focus on shared decision-making, and require museum staff and leadership to step back and listen. These relationships with community organizations are part of an ongoing dialogue with members of this community. And for museums particularly interested in creating collective impact within a community, strategic partnerships are essential. Falk and Juan write, "When museums acknowledge the expertise of community partners, and partners practice respect for what each brings to the table, the result can be powerful, meaningful programs that honor cultural knowledge and link unique communities together" (2016).

The Science Museum of Minnesota and the Nanoscale Informal Science Education Network created the *Collaboration Guide* (McCarty and Herring 2015), a helpful resource for any museum or organization planning to develop successful partnerships. In the guide, they share a summary of key characteristics of successful partnerships—a short list worth reviewing as you begin a new collaboration or as you reflect on your existing partnerships (McCarty and Herring 2015):

1. Be patient! Collaboration takes time. Always keep long-term relationships in mind while working on shorter-term projects.
2. Be clear about your goals and expectations, and ensure your partnership is mutually beneficial.

3. Get to know each other. Each partner has a lot to learn and a lot to offer.
4. Communication is critical! Be flexible, open, and involve more than one contact person to ensure a relationship that can survive changing circumstances.
5. Stay focused on your goals. And don't forget to celebrate your successes!

Finally, as you form these partnerships as well as advisory groups, be sure to involve staff from across your institution as much as possible. Many museums involve only staff from education departments, or staff who are already involved in potential community work. If you are going to build a community of change across your institution, you need to involve staff from curatorial, collections, security, visitor services, marketing, and development, even if some of these departments might feel threatened by consulting with community members. Through embracing a mindset of co-creation and collaboration, all the people of the museum are a valuable part of the process rather than a barrier to being more community centered.

CONCLUSION

Why open up museums to the challenges and potential failures of community-centered work? Why invest the time, staff, energy, and resources it takes to do this work really well? Why take on such risks? Wouldn't it be easier to just keep with business as usual?

When faced with these questions, I find myself going to museum scholar Stephen Weil's befitting statement from his classic book *Making Museums Matter*: "The museum that does not prove an outcome to its community is as socially irresponsible as a business that fails to show a profit. It wastes society's resources" (Weil 2002, 43). As museums and other institutions take steps to embrace community engagement, it is important to understand why this shift is occurring toward working with communities and local residents. In many cases, these changes are primarily motivated by reaching new audiences and market segments for increased ticket sales or visitor numbers. While I am not going to explore this in detail here, many of these arguments for community outreach are centered in decisions that generate benefits for institutions. A core question to ask ourselves is, when we focus on community, are we more concerned "with the revival of community or with the survival of the museum?" (Crooke 2007, 79). As Elizabeth Crooke keenly states, "[W]hen engaging with community, the museum sector does not have an altruistic agenda. Just as people seek community when they are looking for security in an insecure world, museums also pursue community when they need to reassess their roles and their futures" (Crooke 2007, 79). These words echo particularly true as many museums struggle to reimagine themselves given the sweeping effects of the pandemic. If our goal as changemakers is to transform museums into vital members of our communities, then shouldn't we be regularly and consistently taking bold steps to bring community into the heart of our institutions?

The meaning of community requires more thoughtfulness and deliberation than we typically give it. Going forward, museum professionals and leaders must embrace this complexity as they strive to understand and create social change. It is not enough for museums to become an essential part of our communities—our communities also need to become an essential part of our museums. Are we ready to let our community in, as Josh Boykin proclaimed, and allow neighbors, local residents, and community members to shape our practices, programs, and policies? Are we ready to toss out the false barriers between museums and communities?

To reconnect with the words of bell hooks, I invite you to meaningfully reflect on what would it mean for museums and cultural organizations "to be in community, to work in community, and to be changed by community" (hooks 2017). These words can become a type of mantra for changemakers as we work to build more community-centered institutions.

REFERENCES

Block, Peter. 2008. *Community: The Structure of Belonging.* Oakland, CA: Berrett-Koehler.

Brosi, George, and bell hooks. 2012. "The Beloved Community: A Conversation between *bell hooks* and *George Brosi.*" *Appalachian Heritage* 40 (4).

Crimmins, Peter. 2017. "Philadelphia Assembled Marks Finale at Art Museum's Perelman Building." WHYY, December 8, 2017. https://whyy.org/segments/philadelphia-assembled-marks-finale-art-museums-perelman-building.

Crooke, Elizabeth. 2007. *Museums and Community: Ideas, Issues and Challenges.* London: Routledge.

Falk, Lisa, and Jennifer Juan. 2016. "Native Eyes: Honoring the Power of Museum and Community Partnership." American Alliance of Museums. https://aam-us.org/2016/11/09/native-eyes-honoring-the-power-of-museum-and-community-partnership.

Garcia, Stacey Marie. 2012a. "Community and Civic Engagement in Museum Programs: A Community-Driven Program Design for the Santa Cruz Museum of Art & History." MA thesis, Gothenburg University.

———. 2012b. "Guest Post: Community and Civic Engagement in Museum Programs." *Museum 2.0* blog. http://museumtwo.blogspot.com/2012/09/guest-post-community-and-civic.html.

hooks, bell. 1996. *Killing Rage: Ending Racism*. New York: Penguin.

———. 2017. "Building a Community of Love: bell hooks and Thich Nhat Hanh." *Lion's Roar*, March 24, 2017. https://www.lionsroar.com/bell-hooks-and-thich-nhat-hanh-on-building-a-community-of-love.

Institute of Museum and Library Services. 2017. *Strengthening Networks, Sparking Change: Museums and Libraries as Community Catalysts.* https://www.imls.gov/sites/default/files/publications/documents/community-catalyst-report-january-2017.pdf.

———. 2018a. Museums Empowered, FY 2018 Notice of Funding Opportunity. https://www.imls.gov/sites/default/files/fy18-oms-me-nofo.pdf.

———. 2018b. *Transforming Communities: Strategic Plan 2018–2022.* https://www.imls.gov/sites/default/files/publications/documents/imls-strategic-plan-2018-2022.pdf.

Kadoyama, Margaret. 2018. *Museums Involving Communities*. New York: Routledge.

Kavanagh, Gaynor. 1990. *History Curatorship.* Leicester, UK: Leicester University Press.

McCarty, Catherine, and Brad Herring. 2015. *Collaboration Guide for Museums Working with Community Youth-Serving Organizations.* http://nisenet.org.

Mogilevich, Valeria, Mariana Mogilevich, Prerana Reddy, Alexandra García, and José Serrano-McClain. 2016. *Corona Plaza Es Para Todos: Making a Dignified Public Space for Immigrants. Queens Museum.* http://www.queensmuseum.org/wp-content/uploads/2016/01/Corona-Plaza-Es-Para-Todos_web.pdf.

Moore, Porchia. 2015. "R-E-S-P-E-C-T! Church Ladies, Magical Negroes, and Model Minorities: Understanding Inclusion from Community to Communities." *Incluseum* blog. https://incluseum.com/2015/10/15/respect-church-ladies-magical-negroes-model-minorities-inclusion-community-to-communities/

Pfortmüller, Fabian. 2017. "What Does 'Community' Even Mean?" *Medium.* https://medium.com/@pforti/what-does-community-even-mean-a-definition-attempt-conversation-starter-9b443fc523d0.

Putnam, Robert. 2000. *Bowling Alone: The Collapse and Revival of American Community*. New York: Simon and Schuster Paperbacks.

Rajagopalan, Kavitha. 2017. "How a Museum in Queens Became a Neighborhood Ally." *NextCity.* https://nextcity.org/daily/entry/how-a-museum-in-queens-became-a-neighborhood-ally

Salisbury, Stephan. 2017. "Why There's a North Philly Living Room Going on Display at the Art Museum." *Philadelphia Inquirer.* September 7, 2017. https://www.inquirer.com/philly/entertainment/arts/philadelphia-art-museum-philadelphia-assembled-20170907.html

Simon, Nina. 2009. "Eight Other Ways to 'Connect with Community.'" *Museum 2.0* blog. http://museumtwo.blogspot.com/2009/08/eight-other-ways-to-connect-with.html.

———. 2015. "Meditations on Relevance, Part 3: Who Decides What's Relevant?" *Museum 2.0* blog. http://museumtwo.blogspot.com/2015/08/meditations-on-relevance-part-3-who.html.

———. 2016. *The Art of Relevance*. Santa Cruz, CA: Museum 2.0.

Stuart, Graeme, 2018. "What Is Asset-based Community Development (ABCD)?" *Sustaining Community* blog. https://sustainingcommunity.wordpress.com/2013/08/15/what-is-abcd/.

Terruso, Julia. 2017. "Art Museum Puts Gentrification on Center Stage." *Philadelphia Inquirer*, September 7, 2017. https://www.inquirer.com/philly/news/philadelphia-assembled-art-museum-gentrification-20170907.html.

Trouillot, Terrence. 2017. "Tania Bruguera Launches Bike-Based Project to Improve Ties between Immigrants and NYC Government." *ArtNet*, May 30, 2017. https://news.artnet.com/art-world/cyclenews-975428.

Watson, Sheila, ed. 2007. *Museums and Their Communities*. London: Routledge.

Weil, Stephen. 2002. *Making Museums Matter*. Washington, DC: Smithsonian Institution Press.

3

Community at the Core

A Conversation with Nina Simon

As museums and cultural institutions make the shift to become more community-centered, one key changemaker and leader advocating and leading this change has been Nina Simon. Nina most recently served as the Spacemaker and CEO of OF/BY/FOR ALL, a global nonprofit initiative to empower civic and cultural organizations to become of, by, and for their diverse communities. Prior to founding OF/BY/FOR ALL, Nina was the executive director of the Santa Cruz Museum of Art and History (MAH), where she led a dramatic turnaround and eight years of growth rooted in community involvement. She is the best-selling author of *The Participatory Museum* (2010) and *The Art of Relevance* (2016), and has been named an Ashoka fellow, a "museum visionary" by *Smithsonian Magazine*, and Santa Cruz County Woman of the Year. Nina lives off the grid in the Santa Cruz mountains with twenty people, twenty-four chickens, three dogs, and one zipline.

I first met Nina many years ago after the publication of *The Participatory Museum*, and was an avid reader of her *Museum 2.0* blog about museums. I'm fortunate to have had so many conversations with Nina over these years, to visit with her at the MAH, and to be a part of her work with OF/BY/FOR ALL. The following conversation was recorded in December 2019, and explores Nina's work as a changemaker at the MAH and aspects of this work that she continues to learn in her work with OF/BY/FOR ALL and organizations across the globe. Some key learning we discuss in this conversation include:

- The importance of driving change forward across an entire institution, and not just through selected programs or exhibitions
- Thinking of audience members or visitors as collaborators in the work that we do within museums

- Aligning community building work with a museum's broader equity work
- Focusing on an asset-based approach to communities that also pays attention to the external barriers that community members face

Mike: Nina, your work and writings have certainly been influential across the museum field, especially in the realms of participatory practice and transforming museums into more community-centered institutions. I feel like we've been on this journey together in so many ways, and you've been such a valuable colleague, teacher, friend, and mentor. I'm grateful to have been able to visit you and the Santa Cruz Museum of Art and History (MAH) several times during your time there, as part of MuseumCamp and the OF/BY/FOR ALL movement. After visiting the MAH and being out in the Santa Cruz community, I have gained such a deep respect for, appreciation of, and recognition of your work by seeing it happen on the ground, throughout the museum itself and also with individuals and groups across Santa Cruz who are partnering with the museum. You've always been able to push my own practice a bit further and keep that fire burning to bring community into the core of institutions like museums.

I'd love to spend our time together talking a bit more about your passion to change museums, and some ways that museum leaders and changemakers can keep boldly pushing this change forward. To begin, I've always been curious: why museums? Why have you decided to dedicate so much time and energy to making change happen within museums, rather than perhaps working within organizations already embedded in their communities and doing the work?

Nina: I think that I came into museums based on a single data point that turned out to be not very typical of what most museums are, but it has driven a lot of my career. And that was John Falk. I was an electrical engineering student and had thought since I was a kid that I wanted to work for NASA. I was on this path, but I was also always very left brain, right brain. I enjoyed math and science by day and slam poetry by night. Since I was a teenager, I was really interested in nontraditional forms of education and was a big fan of Paulo Freire and John Falk. I started getting curious about other kinds of educational institutions and various forms of alternative learning.

I remember being in my dorm room searching on the internet (before the days of Google), and I found John Falk's writing about museums as places for free choice learning. I thought to myself, "Oh my God, this is it!" I started volunteering and then working at science centers and children's museums, which really live that story and focus on hands-on engagement. In fact, for the first nine years of my career, I never once worked in a museum that put the collection first, put the curator at the top of the pecking order, didn't have a team-based approach, and didn't have a visitor-centered mentality. So this reinforced what I had read in my early encounter with Falk's writings about museums.

Mike: That's interesting that the way you entered into museums was through your interest in nontraditional learning and the writings of Freire and Falk. Before I even knew that museum education was a thing, I was getting my PhD in education and diving deep into nontraditional learning theories and radical pedagogy. Yet, very different from your experience, I entered museum work through getting a job in art museums and experienced quite a clash between the way these museums functioned and my understandings of teaching and learning.

When you took the job at Santa Cruz, I had met you a couple times by that point but you still seemed like a superstar (to a museum nerd like me). You had written *The Participatory Museum* book, and you were going into the director position in Santa Cruz with the mindset that museums can be these participatory places. But pretty quickly, you and your team there became really focused on being more community centered. It was almost like being an engaging, participatory museum was a step toward being an institution that brings the local community into its core. I wonder if you could talk a little bit about what shifted for you and your team.

Nina: I think there are two things that happened. One was a condition of the role I had, and one was a condition of the community I'm in. By being the director, I started to realize that all of these individual participatory techniques, if brought together and repeated again and again across an institution, could set the stage for visitors to have a fundamentally different expectation about what their engagement might be. Previously, I'd done work either as a low-level educator or exhibit developer, inserting individual strategies into a larger museum system. So if you read *The Participatory Museum*, it's about a technique you can use for comment walls or a technique you can use for collaborative partnerships. This was making the assumption that anybody doing this work only has the ability to impact specific projects or specific areas of the institution. So maybe the best you can do is deploy a bunch of these strategies.

When I was writing *The Participatory Museum*, I never even imagined what it would look like if you brought this all together. Yet being the director of the MAH, we could put so many of these things into action and change the way the whole building felt. Maybe the most basic example of this is about comment walls, or "talk back" spaces. If you have a museum or an exhibition

with one area for talk back, people kind of use it as their release zone for anything they need to say to the institution. But if you have a talk back on every
floor or in every exhibition, people start to realize "oh, they really care what
I think" and "they really want to honor what I have to share." I think it leads
to both better content in the talk backs, but it also makes you more likely as
a visitor to get involved with the institution.

So the first thing that changed was realizing that if you put all these things
together in a building, it changes what's possible with your community.
The second thing was being in a smaller community like Santa Cruz. I had
always previously worked in big cities and institutions like the International
Spy Museum, which has about a million visitors a year. I came into writing
The Participatory Museum with a large museum framework. It wasn't until I
started working at the MAH that I realized I could say "hi" to everyone that
comes in the door. I could have a conversation with every visitor today. I
could see someone at the museum one week, and then see them in the grocery
store the next.

Because of this, there started to be an opportunity to engage in a way that
invited our visitors to get more involved with the institution—start to shift
people from visitors into collaborators. I had never lived or worked in a small
enough place that you could have a totally different relationship with people
coming in the doors. And this really matters when you talk about one of the
primary concerns that comes up around community projects: at the end of the
project, what happens to that community relationship? It's one of the biggest
questions I get asked. What I found at the MAH was that if you built a real
relationship in a smaller community, you're going to see that person in other
places and you're going to be able to continue that relationship in other ways.
We have had so many partners who come in and out of different levels of collaboration in a way that has felt very natural to how human relationships go.

Mike: I appreciate what you've said about how partnerships and collaborations really gain from being treated like human relationships. That resonates
with a lot with the work that I engaged in while at the Portland Art Museum
around community partnerships, including establishing a clear set of values
and even changing the name of our department to "Learning and Community
Partnerships." We wanted to just make a bolder statement around how central
trust and relationship building was to our process. And I totally agree that
these relationships can shift in their intensity, kind of like we do with family
and friends and all kinds of different relationships that we have in our lives.

Nina: I think the thing I'm so curious about is how to do this type of work if
you're in a situation where the whole institution is not reinforcing these same

values. If there are potentially different value sets going on with an institution, it seems like you'd have more caveats on that trust building. How do you approach being a representative of an institution that's much bigger than just the values and commitments of your particular department?

Mike: That's an excellent question. I think we're all constantly learning and growing and failing at the same time. One of the things I have learned is the value of having a home base for this work within a larger institution. While it's great to think that institutions might have directors that are like, "This is what we're doing and this is going to be the whole mission," I don't think that is the reality in most larger institutions. If you can create a core team driving this relationship and partnership work forward, you can begin to build a community of change across the institution. I realize that this home base is often in an education or learning department, and I think that makes a lot of sense for this type of human-centered and community-centered work to start there. It just can't stop there. We have to be having conversations and building bridges across our institutions so the work becomes a commitment for our colleagues across departments as well as the director and executive leadership.

One of the things that's really helped support this type of work within many institutions is aligning community partnerships work with equity work. Throughout a lot of my work, we were thinking about how we could not just connect with local residents, but also how do we recognize, celebrate, and invest in those individuals, groups, or collectives who have been excluded from the traditional power structures of the museum. So I think both building a community of change and aligning community building work with an institution's broader equity work can be successful strategies to get more investment across a larger institution. The work is definitely messy and not always perfectly aligned, but it's important to be transparent about that. And it is important to tell your community partners that you want them to be a part of this change and hold institutions accountable along the way.

Nina: In OF/BY/FOR ALL, we use the term "communities of interest" because we feel like there are a lot of problematic elements to defining these communities as having needs or being at a deficit. I feel like we need to find a way to bring positive value to that idea that these are communities that are of interest to us and that are critical to our future.

Mike: I hear what you are saying. I think even when museums adopt a positive asset-based approach, there's still too much of a focus on how they "share" power or "empower" communities. This mindset exists instead of recognizing that there is power that exists outside the museums and maybe there's a way to recognize existing community power, existing community expertise and knowledge. I'm curious of your thoughts around that idea, especially as you've gotten into the OF/BY/FOR ALL work with so many institutions. What have you learned about that power dynamic in the work that you're doing now?

Nina: I've learned a lot about this from my colleagues at OF/BY/FOR ALL, Lauren Benetua and Mateo Mossey, who both come out of community organizing and cultural organizing work in queer communities, communities of color, and indigenous communities. We've been focused on an asset-based approach, but still talking about both assets and needs. And then Mateo brought forward a shift to focusing on assets and barriers. With this approach, there's not a sense of people having assets and needs, but rather that there are communities that have strengths and face barriers. These barriers are external to them as opposed to them being an internal deficit or need.

Mateo recently shared with us an incredible essay by queer Mexican poet Yosimar Reyes, who is undocumented. In the essay, Reyes talks about the idea that undocumented is not his identity, yet he saw how this barrier that he faced could get weaponized by the media, by politicians, and by well-intentioned white people into a deficit that he had. Reyes did not accept taking this external barrier and turning it into an internal weakness. These barriers that we face are not internal and core to who we are. So I think that getting not just to that assets-based perspective, but getting to that perspective of deep understanding about somebody else's power—that is the most meaningful thing we can do.

Mike: Yes. Through so much of this work, we need to be open to the learning and growth that come with building these relationships, listening to more voices from across our communities, recognizing that they are powerful, and working together to remove barriers. Thanks, Nina. I am so grateful to be able to have this conversation with you. Your work continues to inspire me and many others across the field.

REFERENCES

Simon, Nina. 2010. *The Participatory Museum.* Museum 2.0.
———. 2016. *The Art of Relevance.* Museum 2.0.

4

Interrupting White Dominant Culture in Museums

As I sat down to write this chapter, I found myself reflecting on the sometimes frustratingly slow, pain-laden, and capricious path of change for museums, and my own role as a changemaker and accomplice in this work of making change happen—within museums and within our communities. On my desk in front of me sits a towering pile of books on museum change, activism, and inclusive practices, along with a formidable pile of diversity statements and strategic plans that talk about equity and community. Conference after conference and convening after convening have brought to the center themes of equity, inclusion, relevance, community, and audience. There are rapidly growing networks of activists and changemakers, with expanding movements connecting through social actions, events, book clubs, reading lists, online syllabi, and social media hashtags. Yet given all this, why do some of the pivotal changes happening in museums during the past few years feel tenuous and temporary? Why does deep and meaningful change always feel a bit out of reach? Why does each crisis feel like one more excuse to turn the clock back and return to the status quo?

In a 2019 piece by poet, activist, and community organizer Jamara Wakefield titled "Museums Could Be Powerful, Liberatory Spaces if They Let Go of Their Colonial Practices," she powerfully envisions a decolonized future for museums. She writes:

> Museums could be one of our greatest allies in liberation struggles. They have the physical space, the means, and the public confidence to partake in a large scale social movement against colonial powers. Yet they reject this opportunity over and over again. They prefer to remain silent and hide in a world that desperately needs decolonizing. (Wakefield 2019)

One of the things holding museums back from this level of transformative change is a continued unwillingness to challenge the entrenched institutional structures that advance and maintain inequity and oppression. The pervasive hold of white supremacy is arguably one of the single greatest threats to the deep, transformational change that is needed within museums today. It is a threat to racial equity; it is a threat to environmental and economic justice; it is a threat to accessibility and disability justice; it is a threat to the well-being of Black, Latinx, Indigenous, LGBTQIA, and Deaf and Disabled communities, among many others; it is a threat to human dignity; and it is a threat to those who are struggling to see these universal values of equity, justice, and dignity define our new institutional realities. And it is a threat that is largely unacknowledged by white museum professionals and those in positions of power across the field.

I realize that pressing this idea of examining white supremacy and white dominant culture within museum institutions may bring forward some resistance, defensiveness, tension, and complexity. During the work of spreading the Museums Are Not Neutral campaign and message with co-creator La Tanya S. Autry, we have encountered resistance (sometimes staunch, sometimes more subtle) from some museum leaders and thinkers who are unable or unwilling to see, define, and critically reflect on white dominant culture in their institutions. After all, for me, that campaign is so much about the simple yet powerful recognition that what museums take for granted as "neutral," "objective," "normal," "professional," and "high quality" is all part of a system of white supremacy that perpetuates oppression, racism, injustice, and colonialism. Chapter 5 addresses the work of Museums Are Not Neutral more closely through a conversation with La Tanya.

In an interview with *Smithsonian Magazine*, in May 2019, secretary of the Smithsonian Lonnie Bunch was asked what the phrase "museums are not neutral" means to him. He replied:

> It's crucially important for museums to open the veil, of how they do the work they do so that even they understand the complicit biases they carry. They understand the cultural baggage that shapes what we do. (Py-Lieberman and Wolly 2019)

I frequently reference the words of scholar and activist Angela Davis, who, while speaking to a gathering of Ferguson protesters in 2015, stated:

> Any critical engagement with racism requires us to understand the tyranny of the universal. For most of our history the very category "human" has not embraced Black people and people of color. Its abstractness has been colored white and gendered male. (Davis 2016, 87)

White supremacy thrives within this tyranny of the universal, the neutral, the apolitical, the fair and balanced, and the objective. Acknowledging that "museums are not neutral" is a meaningful and urgent step toward gaining awareness of the powerful role that white supremacy and white dominant culture play within museum institutions. It is a crucial step toward recognizing one's own role in questioning it, interrupting it, and being a part of taking transformative action to replace it.

This chapter will guide you through deeper thinking about the role that white dominant culture plays in museums, and the barriers it creates to our work as changemakers. As changemakers, we need to become comfortable recognizing and naming white supremacy and elements of white dominant culture in museums, and work toward dismantling racism in our organizations and in our lives.

DEFINING WHITE DOMINANT CULTURE AND WHITE SUPREMACY

As part of this discussion, I want to bring in some definitions of *white dominant culture* and *white supremacy* that can be helpful for those who are new to these ideas. If you hear these terms and limit their definitions to the acts of militant white nationalists and hate groups marching with torches, then I suggest you pause here and do some homework. Take some time to connect with the wider discourse around this topic. It is important that we get past these reductive associations, and begin to develop more complex and shared understandings. I also recognize that these terms can bring with them strong emotions and connections to a past of trauma, violence, and suffering; and that we may not agree on which terms are best to use in various situations and contexts.

A useful and widely recognized definition of *white dominant culture* comes from the work of Tema Okun and Kenneth Jones on dismantling racism. They describe it as:

> The explicit to subtle ways that the norms, preferences, and fears of white European descended people overwhelmingly shape how we organize our work and institutions, see ourselves and others, interact with one another and with time, and make decisions. (Jones and Okun 2003)

From their collection of writings titled *How We Fight White Supremacy*, Akiba Solomon and Kenrya Rankin write:

> White supremacy defines our current reality. It is not merely a belief that to be White is to be better. It is a political, cultural, and economic system premised

on the subjugation of people who are not White. . . . White supremacy is the
voice in our collective heads that says it makes civilized sense that one group
of people gets to annihilate, enslave, incarcerate, brainwash, torture, sterilize,
breed, and terrorize other people. (Solomon and Rankin 2019, vii)

Through their work on racism, Okun and Jones have also offered up a list of
characteristics that can help us see where white dominant culture is showing
up in our work and in our lives on a regular basis. These include perfection-
ism, a sense of urgency, defensiveness, either/or thinking, a focus on quantity
and valuing measurable goals, discomfort with emotion, a sense of paternalism in decision making, and fear of conflict, just to name a few.

For some of you reading this, these characteristics may be strikingly familiar
and precisely describe your workplace culture. Have you taken a moment to
step back and question some of these norms? How have you been involved in
promoting and advancing this culture? I can say that I have spent much of my
career in management roles without actively questioning and interrupting these
characteristics, playing my own role in maintaining these structures of inequity
without being conscious of the impact. My goal here is not to make this about
blame or guilt (that happens far too often), but rather to invite everyone (especially white people in managerial roles) to recognize where this is showing up
so we can work as part of a collective effort to interrupt and decenter it.

Aspects of white supremacy are showing up every moment of every day in
the museum workplace. It dictates how people hold meetings together, who
is invited to those meetings, who participates, and whose ideas are valued.
It informs how our front-of-house staff and volunteers interact with visitors,
who works in positions that interact with visitors, the types of training they
receive, and who makes decisions about these trainings. It dictates how museum leaders and managers make decisions, who gets to have input into those
decisions, and who is affected by those decisions. It is a controlling force in
how we define *community*, how we work with community partners, what we
value about those partnerships, and how we resource those relationships. It
dictates the words that get written on museum websites and on panels and
labels in the galleries, and who gets to write, edit, and approve those words.
And each and every one of these moments (and thousands more) threatens to
chip away at the humanity of our colleagues of color, visitors of color, and
all those who are not defined within these norms of "whiteness." On top of
this, it erodes the humanity of us white people, too. As Jasmine Syedullah so
perfectly states, whiteness is "a road to nowhere" (Syedullah 2016, 23).

Real harm is being done throughout every nook and cranny of our institutions, and we need to collectively recognize this before we can take actions to
interrupt white dominance. As Gita Gulati-Partee and Maggie Potapchuk state
in their 2014 article on "Paying Attention to White Culture and Privilege":

[N]ot doing this examination means that any equity conversations and work will continue to take place in a larger container that is shaped by the very dynamics that the group aims to change. (Gulati-Partee and Potapchuk 2014, 27)

WHY AM *I* WRITING ABOUT THIS?

I want to be clear here. I understand that I am a product of white dominant culture and a participant in white dominant culture, not just as a white, heterosexual, cisgender, able-bodied man who has held positions of power within museum institutions, but as a human being living and acting in our society. White supremacy is insidious, pervasive, and systemic. It is the air we breathe. It shapes our language, our relationships, our actions, our decisions, and our emotions. It is showing up in my words as I write this, even as I critique it. And while I have made choices to gain awareness of this domineering and harmful culture, it still floods all aspects of my being in this world.

I have chosen to make my messy and mistake-filled learning process more public (throughout the pages of this book as well as my writings and interviews online) not to create harm but rather to recognize these challenges wherever, whenever, and however possible. Throughout my museum career, I have leaned toward questioning the status quo and the "ways things are supposed to be" without necessarily having "the answer." I enjoy the more fluid exchange of ideas, questions, and experiences that we, as a broader collective of changemakers, can bring to these issues. I find that it is important to open up larger and larger conversations about burning issues so that we can grow together as a community of change and work toward building a positive, thriving future for museums. I believe that we must have these difficult and uncomfortable conversations to truly center collective well-being, care, and healing—things that have been and continue to be lacking within museum organizational culture and public practice.

I raise these questions about white supremacy as part of a rapidly expanding group of museum workers, leaders, and advocates for change who see the language of diversity, equity, inclusion, and accessibility spread like wildfire *on the surface* of museums without necessarily seeing the deep institutional transformations that are needed *within* museums. I also raise these questions as someone who has worked within museums that have experienced change as well as the pain and messiness of grappling with these deeper issues.

My own learning has been happening over the course of many years as a contributor in a community of colleagues, mentors, friends, co-workers, and the many teachers in my life. I recognize the long history of museum workers, activists, educators, elders, community leaders, and radical transformers who have fought against white supremacy, and those whom I see as powerful leaders and mentors in current efforts to dismantle racism and change museums (including La Tanya S. Autry, Monica Montgomery, Teressa Raiford, Keonna Hendrick, Porchia Moore, Radiah Harper, Nicole Ivy, Omar Eaton-Martinez, Chris Taylor, Janeen Bryant, nikhil trivedi, Jackie Peterson, Melanie Adams, Joanne Rizzi-Jones, Dina Bailey, PJ Gubatina Policarpio, Stephanie Cunningham, Aleia Brown, Adrianne Russell, Kayleigh Bryant Greenwell, Chaedria LaBouvier, Lacey Wilson, Raven Cook, Deana Dartt, Chieko Phillips, Elisabeth Callihan, Laura Raicovich, Jaclyn Roessel, Cinnamon Catlin-Legutko, Christy Coleman, Aletheia Wittman, Alyssa Greenberg, Margaret Middleton, Toni Wynn, those working on Museum as Site for Social Action [MASS Action], the Museums and Race team, Museum Hue, Museums Respond to Ferguson, Museum Workers Speak, and many others). I am aware of, and grateful for, the deep thinking and action that has already been done around this issue, and that continues to be done today.

TAKING ACTION TO INTERRUPT WHITE SUPREMACY

The work of interrupting and decentering white supremacy can seem overwhelmingly daunting when we're faced with what seems like the insurmountable task of systemic change. Furthermore, there is no easy fix, mandatory training, or simple prepackaged strategy that can wash away these oppressive structures and legacies. As Solomon and Rankin aptly state, "[I]f we had a magic button we could press to end this nightmare, we would have leaned on that bitch long ago" (Solomon and Rankin 2019, x).

One important place to start, especially for white people, is to simply recognize and name when white culture is showing up in the workplace—and accept the discomfort that comes with identifying these moments without resorting to defensiveness. In a widely shared blog post on challenging white dominant culture in nonprofits, Lupe Poblano, project director at CompassPoint, writes, "White leaders . . . need to locate their own cultural whiteness and become aware of how their internalized superiority shows up and how it negatively impacts POC inside their own organization." He continues, "You, leaders within the white-dominant leadership structure, need to be willing to change you *first*" (Poblano 2019).

Gulati-Partee and Potapchuk stress that "putting white culture and privilege on the table is critical to include in racial equity work—and it is fraught with challenges due to the complex manifestations of structural racism" (Gulati-Partee and Potapchuk 2014, 31). For those doing the more transformational work in museums, I know that you feel these challenges each and every day. For most white people, myself included, the larger structures of white supremacy are elusive and invisible until we gain the awareness to see them. And when we do see them more clearly, it feels like a punch in the gut. As Hannah Heller writes in her 2018 article "Working towards White Allyship in Museums":

> [T]hose moments that feel uncomfortable or anxious are exactly the moments to lean in to as an ally. That feeling is your Whiteness being tested and questioned. Start paying attention to the moments that make you pause. (Heller 2018)

Recognizing these characteristics of white dominant culture is a pretty big step for many of us, yet it doesn't end there. Transformative change begins to happen in our institutional cultures when we examine, interrupt, decenter, and replace these harmful and oppressive organizing structures and habits of mind. Okun and Jones offer an entire set of "antidotes" or alternatives that we can pivot toward, moving away from the established norms of white workplace culture. The MASS Action Toolkit also provides an extremely useful discussion of dominant culture, organizational culture, and inclusion in chapter 3 and many other sections of the tool kit (Museum as Site for Social Action 2017).

The BlackSpace Manifesto, created by a collective of Black artists, architects, designers, urbanists, and changemakers working to amplify Black agency, provides a powerful set of practices that turn us away from white supremacy and center new modes of thinking and working based in equity, justice, love, and trust. Principles include "Create Circles, Not Lines," "Be Humble Learners Who Practice Deep Listening," "Center Lived Experiences," and "Celebrate, Catalyze, and Amplify Black Joy" (BlackSpace 2019). I have shared this manifesto with colleagues at several institutions, using this framework to discuss our own roles in pivoting toward the practices and mindsets highlighted through this project.

STRATEGIES FOR CHANGEMAKERS

After taking time to reflect personally and with colleagues about how we might change museum workplace culture, I have developed a set of key practices that can be front and center in our minds as we transform our practice as changemakers each and every day. I am interested in any way we can bring a more regular, daily awareness to white dominant culture and the ways we can collectively work to interrupt and decenter it. The shifts in practice presented here can be used to spark conversation and change within your organization or workplace, or simply use it yourself as a personal reminder to shift your focus and energy away from white supremacy. It's just a start to getting these conversations to happen more frequently in museums and cultural institutions. The language and characteristics used here come from the thinking and writings of Tema Okun, Kenneth Jones, Maggie Potapchuk, BlackSpace Manifesto, Radiah Harper, Hannah Heller, and Kai Monet, all whom have done exceptional work in helping fight against racism and white supremacy.

Identifying and Replacing White Dominant Culture in Museums

Let's work collectively to identify these and other elements of white dominant culture, and work toward dismantling racism in our organizations and in our lives.

- Move from a focus on professional and transactional relationships toward relationships based on trust, care, and shared commitments.
- Move from protecting power to sharing power.
- Move from a culture of overworking to a culture of self-care and community care.
- Move from a competition and struggle for limited resources to a mindset of collaboration and working to share resources.
- Move away from prioritizing only degrees, work experience, and job titles toward a way of recognizing and centering lived experience
- Move from a place of those with power making decisions for others toward a place where we work to include those affected by decisions in the decision-making process.

I intend to remain openhearted in this work, recognizing that I have a lot of learning ahead of me and a lot of listening to do. I'm committed to being a changemaker as well as a catalyst for these challenging conversations because I believe in the future of museums and I know in my heart that we collectively have the courage to change these institutions in deep, transformative ways. As you continue down the path of being a changemaker, keep coming back to the shifts in practice outlined in this chapter and work toward more personal and institutional reflection around these key issues.

I'm going to put an exclamation point on the end of this chapter here by reconnecting with the meaningful words of Jamara Wakefield. She concludes with this:

> For my activist, artist, dreamer friends, and all who believe in another world, the one where our lives matter, our histories matter, our liberation matters: be prepared to fight in this world but never stop imagining liberation for our future selves. We owe this moment to our future selves. (Wakefield 2019)

REFERENCES

BlackSpace. 2019. *BlackSpace Manifesto.* https://www.blackspace.org/manifesto.

Davis, Angela. 2016. *Freedom Is a Constant Struggle.* Chicago: Haymarket.

Gulati-Partee, Gita, and Maggie Potapchuk. 2014. "Paying Attention to White Culture and Privilege: A Missing Link to Advancing Racial Equity." *The Foundation Review* 6 (1).

Heller, Hannah. 2018. "Working Towards White Allyship in Museums." *Viewfinder,* National Art Education Association Museum Education online publication. https://medium.com/viewfinder-reflecting-on-museum-education/working-towards-white-allyship-in-museums-802963e95612.

Jones, Kenneth, and Tema Okun. 2003. *Dismantling Racism: A Workbook for Social Change Groups.* Portland, OR: Western States Center. http://www.dismantlingracism.org/.

Museum as Site for Social Action. 2017. *Museum as Site for Social Action Toolkit.* https://www.museumaction.org/resources.

Poblano, Lupe. 2019. "Challenging White Dominant Culture: Time to Look in the Mirror." *Compass Point* blog. https://www.compasspoint.org/blog/challenging-white-dominant-culture-time-look-mirror.

Py-Lieberman, Beth, and Brian Wolly. 2019. "Lonnie G. Bunch III to Become the Smithsonian's 14th Secretary." *Smithsonian,* May 28, 2019. https://www.smithsonianmag.com/smithsonian-institution/lonnie-bunch-named-smithsonian-secretary-180972291/.

Solomon, Akiba, and Kenrya Rankin. 2019. *How We Fight White Supremacy.* New York: Bold Type.

Syedullah, Jasmine. 2016. "The Abolition of Whiteness." In *Radical Dharma: Talking Race, Love, and Liberation,* by angel Kyodo williams, Lama Rod Owens, and Jasmine Syedullah, 15–24. Berkeley: North Atlantic.

Wakefield, Jamara. 2019. "Museums Could Be Powerful, Liberatory Spaces If They Let Go of Their Colonial Practices." *RaceBaitr,* May 14, 2019. https://racebaitr.com/2019/05/14/museums-could-be-powerful-liberatory-spaces-if-they-let-go-of-their-colonial-practices.

5

Museums Are Not Neutral

A Conversation with La Tanya S. Autry

While much of our work as changemakers can happen within museums, there is also great value in recognizing the role we play as agents of change independent and separate from these institutions. Our professional identities are not limited to the organizations for which we work, and I have been grateful to be involved in several changemaking initiatives and groups working outside the structures of institutions. One of the most influential, for me, has been Museums Are Not Neutral, an initiative that I launched in August 2017 with La Tanya S. Autry that has since become a global advocacy platform working collectively to expose the myth of museum neutrality and demand equity-based transformation across institutions. The initiative began through an online T-shirt campaign and the social media hashtag #Museums AreNotNeutral. In its first three years, the initiative sold more than three thousand shirts, mugs, bags, and masks to people around the entire world, raised nearly $30,000 for social justice organizations and relief funds supporting museum workers during the pandemic, and has engaged more than one million people across social media platforms. This movement continues to grow, bring people together, and demand change happen now.

I first met La Tanya in fall 2016 after we had connected via Twitter, and we've been having conversations ever since about museums, equity, and the urgent need for transformative change. She has organized exhibitions and programming at the Museum of Contemporary Art Cleveland, Yale University Art Gallery, Artspace New Haven, Mississippi Museum of Art, and other institutions. Through her graduate studies at the University of Delaware, where she is completing her PhD in art history, La Tanya has developed expertise in the art of the United States, photography, and museums. Her dissertation, "The Crossroads of Commemoration: Lynching Landscapes in

America," which analyzes how individuals and communities memorialize lynching violence in the built environment, concentrates on the interplay of race, representation, memory, and public space.

The following conversation has been adapted from an interview that La Tanya and I recorded in May 2020 for the Monument Lab podcast with Paul Farber, senior research scholar at the Center for Public Art and Space at the University of Pennsylvania and director of Monument Lab. We recorded this discussion with Paul just a few weeks before the murder of George Floyd by police officers in Minneapolis, Minnesota, which sparked widespread protests against police violence and racial injustices in thousands of cities and towns across the United States and the tearing down of many monuments honoring racist historical figures and individuals. Through this conversation, we talk about how Museums Are Not Neutral started, where this phrase and idea comes from, and what it means to dismantle the myth of neutrality. Some key learnings we discuss in this conversation include:

- Bringing changemakers together into a community and coalition through social media activism and online fundraising projects
- Doing change work independent of and separate from institutions and professional associations
- Emphasizing the work of individuals as agents of change and recognizing the influence of passionate individuals and independently formed groups in making change happen across the museum field

Paul: I want to start by asking you how you met and how you both started working together.

La Tanya: I think we actually met through Twitter years ago—we had both been following each other's work. The first time we talked in person was in 2016 at MASS Action [Museum as Site for Social Action], which is an initiative through the Minneapolis Institute of Art that started working with a bunch of different folks in museums doing social justice work. That was exciting because a lot of times you're connecting with people online but you don't meet them in person, and that was actually a draw for me to go to that event.

Mike: We definitely connected by 2016 because of the work we were both interested in doing. And that MASS Action original convening was just an amazing way for a bunch of people that were doing good work around social justice in museums to get together. I remember having some really good conversations in Minneapolis at that gathering.

Paul: Where did the phrase "Museums Are Not Neutral" come from? Was it part of those conversations?

Mike: I think one really important thing to always note about the phrase "museums are not neutral" is that it isn't something La Tanya and I created. There is a much deeper history and deeper thinking around this idea of museum neutrality. Just look back to the Civil Rights Movement and some of the things that were happening in museums in the 1960s and 1970s. Activists were pushing back against the white supremacy and colonialism of museums that treated a single dominant, Eurocentric cultural narrative as universal. And museum studies scholars have questioned and challenged museum neutrality for decades.

For me, a lot of museum professionals and leading voices in activism and museums have been important in developing these ideas. This includes Adrianne Russell and Aleia Brown who started the #MuseumsRespondToFerguson Twitter hashtag and conversations demanding that museums respond and take a stand after the murder of Michael Brown by police in Ferguson, Missouri. For me, it was so pivotal to see that call for museums to respond and take action regarding these issues that matter to our local communities. I also recognize the work of Monica Montgomery, museum leader and activist, in shaping my own thinking about the social role of museums. Through her role as founding director of the Museum of Impact, Monica not only produced a social justice and arts festival here in Portland called the Upstanders Fest in early 2017, but also curated the Museums Respond pop-up exhibition that accompanied the MuseumNext conference in Portland later that same year.

So there is definitely a deeper history of thinking and action around this phrase "museums are not neutral," and I'm honored to be part of these larger efforts to challenge the myth of museum neutrality. And I really do feel like now, at this moment, our initiative has been able to pull a lot of people around the world together to form communities and really make change happen.

La Tanya: Definitely, what you're saying is so vital. The history is there, from fifty years ago and even before that. For me a lot of the real energy was especially started around 2014 with the #MuseumsRespondToFerguson call and just wondering why museums weren't really responding to a lot of the things going on. There's been a real tide of activities that have been happening since then. With our initiative, Mike and I came together and were thinking "Let's put this on a T-shirt. Let's make a real statement out of it." So our first Museums Are Not Neutral T-shirt campaign started in August 2017, but this phrase and concept has roots that are very deep and tied to so many people's practice and activism.

Paul: When you started sharing the phrase "Museums Are Not Neutral," how did that impact your own work and what sense did you get from other people about sharing this in person or online?

La Tanya: For me, I love the expression because it's simple. It's right to the point. I'm actually wearing one of my Museums Are Not Neutral shirts right now, and I'm really proud to wear it. I do feel like it is, in a way, a type of armor. It's like, this is going to protect me today when I go out there and it lets people know I'm about no nonsense. I'm wearing this message right across my heart and I really mean it. People ask questions about what it means, and then I'm in conversation with them and sometimes it gets really deep, actually.

What's been really exciting to me is to see people all across the world having this conversation through the #MuseumsAreNotNeutral hashtag, and really building energy and mobilizing. People are supporting each other through the hashtag. It's created a conversation point that lets people get in contact with each other. I have often felt alone. It seemed like other people are afraid to speak, maybe they believe the same thing as me, but they're afraid to speak up. And having the hashtag is a way of coming together with other people. People start building collaborations. So, to me, it's been really exciting and it's a great way to build a network, to build a coalition.

Mike: I would agree with so much of what La Tanya has said about how this phrase has started to live in this world through the T-shirt and hashtag. I also think prior to a lot of the current initiatives and hashtags, I felt a little isolated when asking questions and trying to make change in my institutions and then getting resistance. Because a lot of the larger professional associations and a lot of the big institutions just haven't been supportive of these types of conversations around social justice, equity, and transformative change. It was hard to bring a community together.

Just like La Tanya said, as soon as I see someone with a Museums Are Not Neutral T-shirt, it just feels good because you're connected with at least thousands of people all over the world that are really dedicated to pushing and advocating for change and transformation across museums. There are millions of people who have engaged with the #MuseumsAreNotNeutral hashtag on social media. It has become a growing community of support, advocacy, and action, which is so much more powerful than one person trying to do work. I think that this simple phrase has meant so much in terms of recognizing the power that exists among so many museum professionals and people in our communities around the world.

Paul: When you began, did the two of you sit down and make a plan and say, "This is how we're going to deploy this phrase?" Or was it more organic?

La Tanya: That's funny. No, we didn't actually sit down and talk about it. I mean, there was a moment I saw Mike wrote the expression "museums are not neutral" on Twitter, I replied, "Oh, that should be on a T-shirt." We did have a conversation about it, but it's evolved and neither of us had any idea that it would keep going. Originally, I think we both thought this would just be for a couple of months. I didn't realize how important it would be, and I'm really proud of it. But it really became meaningful because other people took it on.

We've been growing with it. While we are producing and shaping the initiative in many ways, we also don't claim to control it. It's what people want it to be. So, a lot of its power is that it is really lateral and people find resonance in it. People working in libraries and archives have even launched their own "archives are not neutral" and "libraries are not neutral" campaigns, which is a really lovely thing to watch and be a part of.

Mike: Yes, and from the beginning, simply just getting involved with this campaign has meant you're doing something to support social justice. The profits from all the product sales go to support social justice charities and nonprofit organizations doing important work. We have supported the Southern Poverty Law Center, the Community Foundation of Greater Flint and the Children's Health Fund, and the Museum Workers Speak Relief Fund that helped support museum professionals in need after the massive layoffs during the pandemic. It has been important to us that this initiative be a part of making a positive change in this world, and we continue to make sure that's a core part of everything we're doing.

Paul: From your perspectives, what are the dangers and pitfalls of trying to find neutrality in a place like a museum?

La Tanya: For me, neutrality has never been something I have ever really valued or wanted to be a part of. So, I always found it to be bizarre that people would have that expression. I've always felt like I didn't need to have a PhD to understand that nothing about a museum is neutral. I already knew that early on as a kid, that none of this was neutral. That neutral claim to me has always been a rhetorical stance—a way to cover up something or shut something down, a position to take that upholds the status quo, which is obviously in itself not neutral.

Mike: So much time, energy, and resources go into propping up this idea of neutrality. I mean, it's just part of the system of white supremacy and patriarchy to support this lie, as La Tanya said. It's just dangerous for so many institutions to be supporting this false idea.

Someone recently told me that they felt that a lot of this activism across museums is taking such a negative approach. They suggested that I must not like museums very much because I'm always so critical of them. But that's not the case, at all. I know museums, I know the potential they have, and they're not living up to it. I know the changes that need to happen. Most museums started as colonial institutions, but I believe they can shed that and make some serious transformations internally and externally. I believe that there is a potential for a very different type of institution. So I think it's worth asking these questions, and exposing, erasing, and replacing this idea of neutrality. I understand that it's really hard to make these changes, but we're seeing that more and more people are committing to having these conversations and asking these questions.

One of the biggest fears that I have right now is that this pandemic is causing a lot of pressures on museums in terms of resources and staff. The cuts that we see museums making right now are likely going to deprioritize a lot of these conversations. We see institutions putting this work on hold, and emphasizing a "return to normal" as they plan to reopen to the public. It just pains me to see what I think might be a return to neutrality as museums try to return to normal throughout this pandemic crisis.

La Tanya: Of course, that return to normal is a return to violence. To me, I'm not actually interested in the normal. I mean, I don't want there to be the pandemic that we have right now, but I'm not interested in returning to the same kind of systems we had in place before things closed down. These systems that we have are violent. People think these diversity, equity, and inclusion activities are things on the side, when in reality they should have always been at the fundamental core of the whole institutional project in the first place. If equity was always centered as a regular part of the institution of museums, we would see things rolling out very differently right now. We shouldn't be trying to return to normal. If anything, this is actually a great time to really be pushing toward what diversity, inclusion, and equity really are supposed to be about within these institutions.

Paul: In this moment, what are you seeing as ways that museum workers are pushing back against that mindset of "return to normal," and instead organizing or envisioning other kinds of work that matches the spirit of your movement?

Mike: Well, I think one big thing is transparency, especially around the ways that museum workers are being affected by the pandemic closures through layoffs, furloughs, and budget cuts. Initiatives like Art and Museum Transparency have created public Google documents that are getting as much information out there as possible, and I think this is a really important form of activism. This form of transparency is vital when it comes to holding museums accountable for their actions and decisions.

Another thing that I'm seeing in terms of how we could potentially reimagine museums going forward is a focus on care and healing. How can institutions be human-centered and think about people first? I've spoken to a few directors of smaller institutions and they're struggling way more than the big institutions. They don't have large endowments. They don't have big donors as much as these large institutions do. And they are not receiving large stimulus support from the federal government right now in the pandemic. But they are the ones in so many cases who are bringing their teams together and saying, "Look, we care about each other and that's what matters most." And we know that's what our community cares about because we represent and reflect our community. There are institutions out there that are thinking about that first right now, and I think larger institutions can learn a lot from them. I think if we can center and build practices around healing, accountability, and care, I really think that's when we can start changing what institutions look like. We can start to change some of these really harmful and violent practices and begin to make a difference.

La Tanya: I love how you're talking about a focus on care. I've definitely seen that with smaller institutions. I also like the equity statement that MASS Action team wrote, highlighting what equity means at this time and calling on institutions to do something like making an equitable pay reduction. It's a really important statement. Of course, if people are actualizing it, that's even better. It's been important to see groups on social media like Art and Museum Transparency putting out really wonderful information and bringing people together. We're seeing people actually organizing and starting to build things.

When people ask me, "Where's the real exciting kind of work happening?" I would say it's important to look at the work being done by individuals rather than work coming out under an institutional directive. I don't think that's where the important, deepest, most authentic work is happening. It's coming from passionate individuals who work at various institutions, and who are coming together and making things happen.

During a recent Twitter conversation hosted by Museums and Race about what the term *radical* means, it was mentioned that we need an organization of museum workers—not just the institutional professional associations like the American Alliance of Museums. A lot of energy and excitement got generated through that conversation. Who knows? Maybe we were going to do something. I think various people have had these thoughts over years that there should be some kind of more umbrella organization. I've seen these various forms of mutual aid organizing that tie to this idea of collective care.

It's like this real love that's happening, of people caring for one another and developing fundraisers to help out colleagues who need to be able to pay their rent, get groceries, pick up prescriptions, things like that. All of this is really powerful and exciting. And a lot of this work, as I said, isn't coming from institutions, it's coming from individuals who are creating collectives because they want to and need to.

Paul: As you point out, we're in a moment where we need a lot of care, a lot of healing, a lot of urgent action. Museums are part of the question of what public space is and will be. If you have a wish or an intention for museums in this moment, what is it? What do you envision is important, sustaining for museums today?

Mike: After talking about how things like neutrality, colonialism, and violence that have been really institutionalized as part of museums, I feel like the opposite—these ideas of healing, care, and humanness—can also be institutionalized to respond to that. I believe that we can build institutions and structures that really start to center equity, community, and care and start to replace some of these old, harmful practices. At the core of all of this is this project of recentering and reimagining institutions all across this country and in the world to become more human-centered, and to connect more deeply with these human values of relationship-building and community.

I use the word *love* more now than I have before. I think people need to look more into what that really means in the work that we're doing and what that could really mean as institutions connect with communities instead of hiding behind their walls at a moment like this. So, I think there is so much potential, possibility, and opportunity. There just needs to be this moment of risk taking to lean toward these ideas of care and healing, and not just retract to prioritize collections, donors, endowments, and the bottom line.

La Tanya: Yes, I would love to see more of that focus on caring about humans, caring about beings, and realizing that we are all interdependent. I think about the idea of the word *curator*, it comes from a Latin and it means "to care." I think many curators think of their job very much as caring for objects, and maybe some think of it as caring for artists. Yet there is this idea of caring for people in general. I like to think of my work as a curator is trying to center care as a praxis, thinking "This is my practice. And this is how I'm hopefully making the world better through my work."

Thinking of curating as caring for our communities. I would love to see museums really embody that and mean it. It would be wonderful if museums became these spaces that cared about community, that cared about people at least as much as they care about the objects in their collections. I would love to see a real caring for all people.

6

Leading toward a Different Future

Since the beginning of the COVID-19 pandemic and throughout the ongoing protests demanding racial justice, we have seen evidence of a wide range of leadership qualities on the public stage—watching national political leaders on TV and through social media, seeing governors and mayors respond to these crises in their own states and cities, and feeling the effects of how those leading our museums and nonprofits have decided to respond. The behaviors of those in traditionally defined leadership positions have varied from being fairly brave, vulnerable, and serving the greater good, to acting in ways that are extremely harmful, self-serving, violent, and reprehensible. For museums, we've certainly seen this full range of leadership behavior—unfortunately, far too much of the self-serving, harmful kind.

Leadership at institutions including the Philadelphia Museum of Art, the Guggenheim, the Museum of Modern Art, the Detroit Institute of Arts, the San Francisco Museum of Modern Art, the Getty, the New Orleans Museum of Art, Newfields (formerly the Indianapolis Museum of Art), and countless other museums have been called out for their inequitable and opaque decisions to cut and furlough staff; for actions taken to prevent staff from organizing and forming unions; for their role in creating and perpetuating toxic and racist work environments; for sexual harassment and abusive behavior toward staff; for censoring staff and community voices; and for unethical behaviors regarding collections practices, hiring practices, and artwork loan practices. In a few cases so far, demands for accountability from staff, former staff, artists, and community members have led to action—the executive director of the Museum of Contemporary Art Cleveland resigned amid calls for new leadership, and the executive director and chief curator of the Museum of Contemporary Art in Detroit was forced to resign after charges of racism and abuse. In Canada, the president and CEO of the Canadian Museum for Human Rights was forced to step down because of accusations of censorship, racism, and sexual harassment. And the Detroit Institute of Arts Staff Action group called for the resignation of the executive director amid a whistle-blower complaint filed with the state of Michigan and the Internal Revenue Service along with claims of a hostile and chaotic work environment at that institution under his leadership.

These are not isolated examples; rather, these behaviors are indicative of a field-wide crisis in leadership—a crisis that has existed for too long, yet has been exposed through more recent efforts to increase transparency, organize and take collective action, and hold institutions and those in positions of power accountable. As curator, writer, and activist Kayleigh Bryant-Greenwell calls out in a recent open letter for Museum as Site for Social Action (MASS Action):

> For far too long our field has been led exclusively by white, cisgendered, male, privileged, overly educated, wealthy, elite, upperclass, heteronormative, ableist, colonist gatekeepers. (Bryant-Greenwell 2020)

UPENDING OUR IDEAS ABOUT LEADERSHIP

The prevailing notion of leadership has been defined through existing white, patriarchal norms of power, authority, and control as well as the systems of oppression and domination that are so entrenched in museums. When we use the words *leader* and *leadership*, we are too often only thinking of the single person at the top, the "boss," an individual who simply holds a job title with words like *director*, *chief*, *head*, *president*, *executive*, or *chair*. In a 2017 article for *Nonprofit Quarterly*, the co-founder of the Nonprofit Democracy Network Simon Mont writes, "We have built our organizations around an idea that our leadership should come from either a single individual or a small group," pointing out the urgent need for this outdated, individual-centered understanding of leadership to be replaced. In addition to this narrow idea of top-down decision making, many museums and nonprofits are also replete with poor communication, lack of transparency, overly hierarchical structures, and a distinct unwillingness to change. This all results in the further marginalization of Black, Indigenous, Latinx, Deaf, Disabled, and LGBTQIA staff, volunteers, and audiences. "The dominant organizational structure of nonprofits," Mont declares, "is unsustainable" (Mont 2017).

In her post, Bryant-Greenwell contends that "our museums reflect our leadership." If, indeed, our museums reflect these behaviors and this broken model of leadership, then museums are certainly in a heightened moment of crisis and concern—which only feels more urgent when paired with the sweeping effects of the pandemic on these institutions and their staff.

Yet with each and every crisis comes a possibility for change.

In the Center for Cultural Power's guide on cultural activism during the pandemic, co-founder and president Favianna Rodriguez reflects that "in moments of disillusion and fractures, there is also an opportunity to sow ideas for a different kind of future" (Treibitz et al. 2020).

Now, more than ever, is the time for us to upend our conventional ideas about leadership and what it means to be a leader; to rethink what it means to bring people together for a collective purpose and shared vision; and to redefine what values and skills are truly necessary to navigate our current crises and shape the future of museums. It is up to all of us to choose to embrace a "different kind of future."

REFLECTING ON LEADERSHIP

After the pandemic began closing museums in March 2020, I spent quite a bit of time taking a step back to reflect on this idea of "leadership" and what it means for museums specifically. While writing this chapter during the spring and summer of 2020, I participated in a reading group on "leadership in times of crisis" facilitated by the Radical Support Collective; I read through piles of articles and several key books on leadership and organizational structures, and I spoke with many people who hold leadership positions within organizations or whom I would define as leaders in the field of museums (even though their institutions have not recognized them as such).

Leadership is something I have consistently thought about in each and every institution I have worked for, experiencing a wide array of leadership styles while also working to shape my own practice of leadership. I have seen and experienced instances of both courageous and paltry leadership, and I have no doubt been the purveyor of such experiences to those reporting to me over the years. Through all of this, I have regularly asked myself: What does leadership look like? What should leadership look like? External pressures and expectations be damned. What does being a leader mean for me?

Over the past several years, ideas of care, healing, and collective well-being have become core to my own personal practice of being an educator, team member, advocate, change agent, and leader. In so many ways, these values have been shaped by and with others that I have worked alongside, whether in the same department, across different areas of the same institution, or as part of the amazing groups and individuals around the United States and world advocating for workers' rights, demanding equity, and pushing forward a more community-centered and people-centered vision for museums. So as

the pandemic hit and I found myself among the thousands of museum workers being laid off from their institutions, these core values have been like my
bedrock, my guiding light, my North Star.

Which is why I was really struck by an article written in April 2020 by
Kathleen Osta, managing director of the National Equity Project. In her piece,
titled "Leading through the Portal to Claim Our Humanity," she frames the
pandemic-induced moment of heightened anxiety and uncertainty as a "once
in a lifetime opportunity to increase our global empathy—to practice radical
compassion—and to pay attention to our collective well-being." That has
resonated with me in such a strong way, especially in my thinking about how
we can use this moment to shift our vision of leadership. Osta writes:

> How might we use this global crisis to re-order our priorities and lives in ways
> that increase our collective well-being? . . . How might we organize our lives at
> the interpersonal level and lead change at the institutional and structural level
> with the awareness that we belong to each other—that every human being is
> worthy of our attention and care? What might be possible for ourselves and for
> future generations if we decide to live and lead with this value? (Osta 2020)

RETHINKING LEADERSHIP

I propose that we use this incredibly unique and unprecedented moment—and
the future beyond—to seriously rethink what leadership means, and replace
worn-out, conventional ideas with new possibilities. For me, among the vast
and deep thinking out there about leadership, there are three key principles
worth exploring here:

- Leadership is human centered.
- Leadership means challenging existing hierarchies.
- Leadership is a collaborative, collective, and shared endeavor.

While I don't pretend that any of these ideas are new, I certainly wish I had
come across them much earlier in my own career; and I think working for
leaders who more closely embodied these principles would have significantly
changed my work within museums, my ongoing relationship to these institutions, and their overall response to the crises of COVID-19 and racial injustice. I see the powerful role that white supremacy, capitalism, and patriarchy
have played in developing the accepted traditions and destructive politics of
leadership, and what kinds of leadership traits we have been taught to value
and which traits we have been taught to actively devalue. Yet it is past time
that we unsettle and challenge these norms, demand change from those who

hold positions of power and authority, and build a future that celebrates and centers care, collaboration, belonging, and well-being.

LEADING MEANS BEING MORE HUMAN

In an April 2020 conversation with *New York Times* columnist Thomas Friedman about leadership in times of crisis, business expert Dov Seidman stressed the need for leaders to put people ahead of profits and heed the call to pivot in ways that are anchored in "deep human values." Seidman ends the exchange by saying, "Leaders who in this pause hear that call . . . will be the ones that will earn our most enduring respect and support" (Friedman 2020). I found it worth noting that as the initial economic effects of the pandemic hit, Seidman was tapping into something that most museum directors and boards were not: the importance of people—and, I would add, the deeply human values that lead us to care for each other first, before we panic and obsess about the bottom line.

Since the grim picture of revenue loss and budget shortfalls became apparent for many museums during the COVID-19 pandemic—especially for larger institutions—we have repeatedly seen people in leadership positions deciding to prioritize balanced spreadsheets and protect endowments over connecting with and supporting the people who make up their organizations. I see this as indicative of the problems with leadership that I outline here, a model of leadership in which the decisions of one person (or a small few) are based in a desire to preserve power and authority.

Counter to this, I have spoken with a few directors at institutions faced with the same financial problems who have nonetheless refused to lay off staff. The reason for this, one director said, was because "it didn't feel like the human thing to do." They were willing to be more human at a time when those following the traditions of leadership were protecting themselves, hoarding power, and hiding behind hollow public relations statements. They were refusing to perpetuate harm at a time when trauma was all around us.

During the Radical Support Collective's four-week reading group on "leadership in times of crisis" that I was a part of in April 2020, we read *Who Do We Choose to Be?* by Margaret Wheatley, a teacher and leadership consultant best known for her classic 1992 text *Leadership and the New Science*. While I still have many questions about Wheatley's thoughts on leadership, one quote early in *Who Do We Choose to Be?* resonated with me in that particular moment. Her words have helped me understand the vital importance of transforming leadership, specifically as part of the work to change museums. She writes:

> I know it is possible for leaders to use their power and influence, their insight and compassion, to lead people back to an understanding of who we are as human beings, to create the conditions for our basic human qualities of generosity, contribution, community, and love to be evoked no matter what. (Wheatley 2017, 8)

Embracing a human-centered mindset in museums asks us to elevate care, relationship building, and collective well-being as integral elements to our institutions' values and culture. It is about putting all human beings (not just visitors or audiences) at the center of our organizational thinking rather than collections, big donors, endowments, curatorial silos, or shiny capital projects. For those in leadership positions, I think this means setting aside ego, stepping back, learning to listen in radical ways, and making decisions based in care and deeply held human values—and doing this all while it runs counter to conventional thinking, entrenched legacies of leadership, and the expectations of funders.

In his book *Reboot: Leadership and the Art of Growing Up*, leadership development expert and executive coach Jerry Colonna writes about how the habits and behavioral patterns of CEOs have been detrimental to their own well-being and the well-being of others. On page one, he states:

> I believe that better humans make better leaders. I further believe that the process of learning to lead well can help us become better humans. (Colonna 2019, 1)

In my copy of Colonna's book, these two sentences are heavily underlined. I remember reading this for the very first time, and just sitting with it. I was in the middle of a particularly challenging decision, and I was looking for guidance on how to move forward. Much of Colonna's book and practice is focused on radical self-inquiry and finding ways to listen deeply to our own hearts. I thought about how white dominant culture and traditional gender norms teach us to resist this vulnerability and instead put up a façade of confidence and decisiveness. Make the decision, stand by it, get back to work, and move on.

Being a more human-centered leader—and leading from a place of deeper human values—requires us to resist this pressure to perform the rigid expectations of "leadership" that are harmful. It requires us to slow down and ask ourselves a series of meaningful questions:

- What is my work to become a better human?
- What is my own power and privilege within society and within the structures of this institution?

- In what ways have I been making decisions based on the norms and expectations of a toxic workplace culture?
- How am I complicit in creating or reinforcing the conditions of a toxic work culture?
- How can I break free from existing and traditional expectations, and lead from my heart and from a place of humanness—despite the risks or consequences?

After all, as Colonna writes, "Power in the hands of one afraid or unwilling to look into the mirror perpetuates an often silent, always seething violence in the workplace" (Colonna 2019, 181). This process of self-inquiry is ongoing, and we need to practice holding space for qualities such as care, compassion, healing, deep listening, emotional maturity, and a sense of interconnectedness with other human beings and with our planet. It is a practice that we can cultivate and grow through journaling, meditation, mindfulness, dialogue with others, building a community of support with those who truly value these qualities, and learning from work being done outside the field of museums in social justice, restorative justice, community organizing, nonviolent communication, climate activism, and healing practice. These are not "soft" skills, as they have frequently been referred to as a way to write off and devalue them. These are essential skills. At a time when our society is in urgent need of care and healing, being a more human-centered leader means making a commitment to create the conditions for these qualities—and the individuals who uphold these qualities—to thrive.

Some of you might be having trouble processing how any of this relates to leadership (or, at least, the ideas of leadership you've held dear for so long). Or you might be thinking that, while this all sounds nice, it is just not practical within the "reality" of an organization. You might even be thinking to yourself: I get all of this, but will my employees and team respect me if I am more vulnerable and more human?

You are not alone. The entire construction of "effective leadership" in our minds has been built up by the systems of white supremacy, patriarchy, and corporate capitalism. So it makes some sense that you are feeling resistance to any suggestion that you uproot these entrenched ideas. But trust me, let your reticence and resistance go. Open yourself to new ways of doing things. Not only are these outdated norms of leadership holding your organization back, but they are harmful to you, those you work with, and the communities you are aiming to build connections with. Ask yourself why unfixing and rethinking your ideas about leadership makes you uncomfortable or defensive. What might be causing you to be fearful of change, in both a personal sense and an organizational sense? What is the worst thing that will happen if you make a commitment right now to being a more human leader?

CHALLENGING THE HIERARCHY

> When will we acknowledge that Western, primarily North American, influenced leadership paradigms are not fit for purpose in the twenty-first century? Our models are failing the world badly. (Stefani 2019, 191)

As I work to rethink and redefine my own ideas of leadership in ways that are more human, more collaborative, and more equitable, I've begun to interrogate the terminologies we commonly use to define a leader as such. Commonly used language for leadership is based on Western frameworks of racial, gendered, colonial, and economic power. Because established notions of leadership are very top-down and individual-centered, words like *leadership* and *leader* have simply become a reference to the people in positions at the top of an organization. Notably, within this hierarchical structure, those with privilege, wealth, and access to established systems of power are the individuals elevated and promoted most.

This terminological framework has played a role in the crisis of leadership because it has conditioned us to affiliate leadership with systems that harm— instead of help—the broader community. It sets a low bar for what leadership can and should be. If leaders are merely those in executive positions and not those with specific qualities, then why wouldn't they fail us time and time again? It's no wonder that we have a crisis in leadership if we rely on such narrow and oppressive models of leadership to begin with.

I suggest we think of leadership a different way—as one disentangled from the language and privilege of hierarchy. I believe we need to put to rest right here and now the idea that leaders only exist at the top in a role perpetually created for a single individual. Rather than continuing to refer to directors and chief executives as *leaders* by default, I suggest we simply refer to them as "individuals in positions of authority" or "those in positions at the top of an organization's hierarchy." That way we can separate these concepts and begin to reimagine leadership through a framework that can prepare us for the future that lies ahead.

During an interview with Bill Moyers in 2007, activist and community organizer Grace Lee Boggs was asked about the leaders of a new movement for social change here in the United States. Boggs responded, "I think we have to rethink the concept of 'leader'" and "embrace the idea that we are the leaders we've been looking for" (Bill Moyers Journal 2007). Through her work advocating for social justice and building a movement of social change,

Boggs defined the ideal organizational structure as one that developed every member as a leader, resisting the conventional notion of having one charismatic leader at the top. She consistently advocated for a more horizontal concept of leadership rather than a vertical one. For her, this idea was a vital part of tearing down the old structures of power and domination, and challenging the hierarchy.

In arts organizations and nonprofits across this country, we have begun to see a shift away from these traditional models of hierarchy and toward more collaborative and collective forms of leadership. These alternatives to top-down hierarchy rely heavily on trust and mutual advocacy, and they work to challenge the structures that have conditioned us to think in the hierarchical way.

> Society has tended to mystify leadership skills as somehow belonging only to a few people who are then seen as better than everybody else. But if we view leadership skills as something that many people have to varying degrees—skills that can be built upon, supported, and enhanced because they are needed in the world, not in order to make one person superior—then we might have a better way of dealing with leadership. (National Dialogue on Educating Women for Leadership, cited in Batliwala 2008, 16)

ADOPTING FORMS OF COLLABORATIVE AND SHARED LEADERSHIP

If the current moment is indeed a unique and unprecedented opportunity for museums to reimagine themselves and emerge as more human-centered institutions, then I cannot think of a better time to seriously consider adopting a collaborative and shared approach to leadership. Not only do collaborative forms of leadership align more strongly with organizational cultures working to advance equity and antiracism, but it is also increasingly difficult for any single individual to possess all of the skills and abilities needed to lead a complex organization into a future of postpandemic uncertainties.

In his post titled "Museum Leadership for the Rest of Us," Robert Weisberg cites a roundtable conversation among business experts and senior partners at McKinsey that calls into question the hero mentality of directors and CEOs in times of crisis. When asked, "Does this mean we are seeing the end of the hero CEO?" Bill Schaninger responded:

> [W]e've seen COVID-19 accelerating the shift away from classic authoritarian leadership to new forms of distributed decision making. . . . CEOs still trying to hold on to top-down mandates could very quickly become the impediment rather than the solution. (Weisberg 2020)

A small number of museums have moved toward various forms of collaborative leadership, although examples are still difficult to come by and there are very few sustained or permanent commitments to these alternative forms of leadership. After a lengthy search, I was able to find a few examples to note:

- Beginning in 2016, Deyan Sudjic and Alice Black served in co-director roles at the Design Museum in London. Both individuals stepped down from these roles in January 2020, and the institution appointed Tim Marlow in a solo director role as well as the first person to serve as chief executive officer.
- The Five Oaks Museum (previously the Washington County Museum) transitioned from a single director to a co-director model in 2019 with the promotion of Molly Alloy and Nathanael Andreini in its first co-director roles.
- At the Fort Collins Museum of Discovery, an organizational merger back in 2008 led to a unique dual leadership model based in a public–private partnership structure. Cheryl Donaldson and Laura Valdez currently serve as co-executive directors of the museum, a model grounded in a partnership relationship and based in co-expertise.
- The Museum of New Zealand Te Papa Tongarewa (Te Papa) established a dual leadership model when it was founded in the 1990s. The partnership between the chief executive officer and Kaihautū (Māori leader) reflects the bicultural nature of the museum. Te Papa acknowledges the unique position of Māori in Aotearoa New Zealand and the need to secure their participation in the governance, management, and operation of the museum. Arapata Hakiwai has served in the role of Kaihautū since 2013, while Courtney Johnston more recently entered the role of chief executive officer in December 2019.
- In September 2020, Birmingham Museums Trust announced its decision to bring Sara Wajid and Zak Mensah on as joint CEOs.

Apart from museums, there are many nonprofits and arts organizations adopting a shared leadership or co-directorship model. A 2017 article in *Nonprofit Quarterly* shared insights from five leading nonprofits that have developed shared leadership structures, including the Building Movement Project, Management Assistance Group, and the Rockwood Leadership Institute (Bell, Cubias, and Johnson, 2017). Arts nonprofit Fractured Atlas has been operating with a shared, nonhierarchical leadership model since 2018, using a moment of leadership transition to experiment with new organizational structures. Fractured Atlas began this new approach with a four-person leadership team, and they have written extensively about their experiences with this model thus far via their blog.

After studying the literature on the topic along with the experiences of those successfully implementing collaborative and shared leadership models, several key benefits appear to emerge.

1. Leads to More Effective Decision-Making

When it comes to decision-making, a collaborative leadership approach focuses more on quality than efficiency. Making decisions may take more time, but this process brings in more perspectives and ideas and results in doing things better collectively. With this process also comes greater transparency as more individuals and staff are involved in making decisions and talking through ideas. In his study titled "Shared Leadership: Is It Time for a Change?" Michael Kocolowski found that organizations identified several benefits of shared leadership, including the "synergy and expertise derived from shared leadership" and "diversity of thought in decision making" (Kocolowski 2010, 27).

In 2019, Cheryl Donaldson and Donna Jared, then co-executive directors at the Fort Collins Museum of Discovery, reflected on some of the keys to making co-leadership work. For them, this model means that co-leaders are bringing their own expertise to the organization and the daily decisions that are made. While each has some autonomous responsibilities, they note that "the lines are blurred, on purpose, to allow us to support one another, to bring different perspectives to decision making, and to hold each other accountable" (Stilwell 2019). According to Tim Cynova, a member of Fractured Atlas's co-leadership team, their shared leadership model "lessens the organization's dependence on any one person, and strengthens strategic thinking and decision-making capacity across a broad range of staff members" (Cynova 2018). When there is more than one leader—and when leadership becomes part of organizational culture—it becomes even more critical to spend a lot of time thinking together, sharing ideas, communicating, and being as transparent as possible.

2. Cultivates Innovation and Growth

For many organizations adopting collaborative and shared leadership models, there is an observed increase in innovation and experimentation. Kocolowski observed that "flow and creativity seem to flourish in a shared leadership environment" (Kocolowski 2010, 27), and that such shared leadership models are particularly important for the growth and development of new ventures and projects. "Co-leadership allows you to think bigger and dream knowing you have a thought partner to dream with," noted Donaldson and Jared at the Fort Collins Museum of Discovery (Stilwell 2019).

In a traditional top-down leadership model, there is often a sense that the knowledge, expertise, and ideas of those at the very top are more valued and important. This way of siloing and isolating innovation in a single leader or small group of managers can work to prevent an organization from truly reaching its potential. A collaborative organization aims to unlock the knowledge, lived experiences, and creative capacities of its entire team, breaking down the barriers that prevent new ideas from bubbling to the surface. As Darlene Nipper of the Rockwood Leadership Institute puts it, "What we're able to accomplish together is way more than I believe any one person could accomplish" (Bell, Cubias, and Johnson 2017).

3. Centers the Value of Relationships

A shared leadership model brings attention to the relational and collaborative aspects of work as well as the ways in which the value of relationship itself can be incorporated into the leadership structures of an organization. As social justice activist and author adrienne maree brown proclaims in her book *Emergent Strategy*, "Relationships are everything" (brown 2017, 28), and the depth of those relationships determines the strength of a system or organization.

Many in co-directorship roles develop a strong sense of connection, respect, and mutual trust with their counterpart. For these models to work effectively, an organization needs to center these values and understand the importance of relationships within organizational culture. Donaldson and Jared reflect about their experience at the Fort Collins Museum of Discovery: "As co-leaders, we've come to understand it is the partnership relationship that is leading the institution, not us an individuals" (Stilwell 2019).

4. Promotes Shared Leadership across the Organization

"Shared leadership does really work, and when it's working well, it's not just about the few people who are codirectors, it's actually about the whole organization," states Susan Misra, co-director at the Management Assistance Group (Bell, Cubias, and Johnson 2017). Collaborative leadership is not just about the individual leaders sharing power and working together—it is also about changing organizational culture and mindset to be more collaborative. For most organizations successfully adopting a shared leadership model, developing a co-directorship is just the beginning of a longer process of building collective structures and new ways of working that include the voices of all staff. Erin Matson, co-director of Reproaction, acknowledges, "The co-directorship model is a powerful way to expand the leadership capabilities of your organization" (Reprojobs 2020).

For Donaldson and Jared, their co-leadership approach at the Fort Collins Museum of Discovery models a flattening out of the organizational chart. They expanded their shared leadership approach to include director-level staff who are invited to work together as a shared group rather than only oversee their own specific departments or areas. Other organizations, including Fractured Atlas and the Five Oaks Museum, have used this moment of collaborative leadership to also deeply explore pay equity and transparency. When organizations take this approach, leadership growth can occur across an entire team and begin to have a powerful effect on many areas of work and practice.

5. Aligns with Antiracism and Equity

With collaborative leadership comes the opportunity to examine what power looks like within your organization and to reimagine how it operates in more equitable and inclusive ways. For some organizations, the shift to co-directorship emerges during a transition out of a particularly oppressive situation with traditional leadership. Overall, a top-down, individualistic model of leadership is in direct contradiction with efforts to advance equity, inclusion, and antiracism. In their discussion with CompassPoint team members about shared power, co-directors of several social justice–focused nonprofits noted that forms of traditional, hierarchical leadership just did not align with the work they do as organizations (Bell, Cubias, and Johnson 2017).

As noted in *Leadership and Race: How to Develop and Support Leadership that Contributes to Racial Justice*, a report developed through a research initiative of the Leadership Learning Community:

> We often reward people whose leadership style is aligned with the individual model of the dominant culture, but not those who engage in more collective forms of leadership. This serves to render invisible the leadership of many women and people of different races/ethnicities. (Keleher et al. 2010, 5)

The report's authors continue:

> Leadership can play a critical role in either contributing to racial justice or reinforcing prevailing patterns of racial inequality and exclusion. . . . To achieve racial and social justice, we need to move beyond the emphasis on the power of individuals to a philosophy of interdependence and building connections. (Keleher et al. 2010, 3, 7)

Fractured Atlas board members Christopher Mackie and Russell Willis Taylor state that the shared leadership model in their organization makes "a powerful statement against the inevitability of hierarchy and the racist, sexist, and otherwise oppressive social institutions and organizations that it enables" (Mackie and Taylor 2020). For Fractured Atlas, their nonhierarchical leadership team helps advance their core values of antiracism and antioppression by modeling an inclusive approach that fosters a diversity of voices, perspectives, and skills. By questioning and breaking away from the commonly accepted ideas of leadership based in white dominant culture, organizations can move toward more inclusive forms of decision-making, collaborative practice, and collective workplace culture.

TAKING ACTION TO BUILD A DIFFERENT FUTURE

In her June 2020 article "On the Limits of Care and Knowledge," Yesomi Umolu, director and curator of Logan Center Exhibitions at the University of Chicago, sharply highlighted the broken foundations of colonial violence and exclusion for museums, writing: "[A]t a time when many civic institutions are being exposed for negligence of duty, museums must recognize their shortcomings and develop new ways of thinking and doing" (Umolu 2020). By replacing the outdated, broken, and harmful structures of leadership and organizational hierarchy, we have the potential to reinvent museums as vibrant, thriving, equitable institutions that are better equipped to navigate the unprecedented challenges of our times and more fully care for their staff and their local communities. Yet nothing is going to change unless we question our assumptions, fight against the entrenched barriers of the status quo and the "we can't" mentality, and begin to take action to make change happen. Beyond the work already discussed in this chapter, here are some additional strategies and actions to help begin this transformation in your own work and in the institutions with which you work.

Celebrate and Elevate Human Values

As I discuss earlier in this chapter, leading means being more human. Radical self-inquiry is an essential practice to uncover what you value and what you stand for, not just as a director, a manager, or an employee but as a human being. Build your own leadership practice by taking the time to learn more about yourself. Find ways to talk to others in your workplace about your values, and make space to surface these together as individuals and as a group. In our culture of productivity dictated by capitalism and white dominant culture, these types of exercises can often be devalued as "pointless" or a "waste of time." It is up to you to make space for these meaningful conversations and time for reflection.

Work toward creating a human-centered workplace culture (in your own team, your own department, and eventually across the institution) that celebrates and elevates deeply human values and brings a focus to care, well-being, and relationship building. And don't just talk about these values—embody them in your own work and in your own leadership. Speak up and connect with others willing to champion these values in your institution and in your life.

For me, one of the most meaningful and memorable sentences in Jerry Colonna's book *Reboot* is this (and I have it written down in several places in my current work space):

> Remember who you are, what you believe about the world, and then, risks be damned, lead from that place of broken-open-hearted warriorship. (Colonna 2019, 102)

Hold Those in Positions of Power Accountable

If there is going to be any real shift in leadership within the field of museums and an emphasis on advancing positive change in communities, it's going to have to come with a sizeable shift in the people who occupy positions of power within these institutions. Whether those individuals begin to listen more fully to their staff and communities and become part of the change that is needed, or whether those individuals transition out of these roles to allow new leaders to emerge, there is an urgent transformation needed at the top level of so many museum organizations. Accountability is a powerful tool to make this change happen, and it is our responsibility (each and every one of us) to relentlessly hold those in positions of power accountable for their actions and behaviors.

During 2020 alone, we've seen efforts from Art + Museum Transparency, MASS Action, Museums Are Not Neutral, Museum Workers Speak, staff organizing groups, museum unions, community members, and many individuals to bring accountability to the forefront. These forms of public accountability can have a powerful effect on institutional change efforts, and at the moment I'm writing this chapter, we've already seen several museum directors forced out of their positions because of these organizing efforts and actions. At many other institutions, the conversations in leadership circles and at the board level have also shifted, considering how to more substantively address the concerns of community members around issues of transparency, ethics, equity, and social responsibility. Stand up, speak up, and become a part of these growing efforts to hold these institutions and those in charge accountable. You can get involved with the many existing campaigns and organizing efforts, reach out to others for support and guidance, and even get something started in your institution or community. And, if the best were possible, those in positions of power and authority can cultivate their own sense of accountability in this work, and we can learn to hold space for that. As peace activist and community organizer Kazu Haga says, ultimately, "accountability is an act of love" (Haga 2020, 131).

Rethink Hierarchies

Part of advancing this shift in thinking about leadership requires us to question, remap, and reimagine the hierarchies of our institutions. In organizations that are dedicated to advancing equity (or working toward moving in that direction), we should be asking how the internal structures and hierarchies can be changed to align with those goals. One way to begin this work is to break down the traditional organizational charts and instead think more about functional and relational connections among team members. This is frequently called "relationship mapping" or "relational mapping."

During a workshop I have facilitated on changemaking within museums and nonprofits, I've asked participants to map out their organizational structures based on the relationships, collaborations, and human connections—tossing out the oppressive, power-centered, top-down "org chart" idea that gets stuck in our heads. While these more human-centered ways to map out our work might seem messy and unstructured, it's important to hold space for these new ways of visualizing organizational structures and let go of habitualized mindsets based in top-down org charts.

It is also important to visually map out power relations and dynamics within an organization, with special attention being paid to who holds power and where there are power imbalances and inequities. Consider individual, social, institutional, and systemic forms of power as well as one's access to resources and the ability to make decisions. Use this process to explore how dominant power structures affect individuals and their relationships with each other. While this can be a challenging exercise that uncovers uncomfortable and even painful truths, revealing the hidden power dynamics at work within an organization is a key part of the work required to challenge old hierarchies.

Both of these types of mapping and charting activities can lead to meaningful conversations and transformative action within an organization around leadership, workplace culture, and equity. The result is a very different way of thinking about how people are interconnected and the relational aspects of our work that are erased and negated through dominant structures of power. This paves the way for seeing leadership being developed, practiced, and supported in new ways across an entire organization, not just at the top.

Publicly and Openly Embrace New Thinking about Leadership

This might sound simple and obvious, but it's also extremely important. As you and your organization begin to rethink leadership and try new ways of doing things, remember to share and celebrate this work publicly (especially if the process has been challenging). We all need to be learning from each other throughout these necessary transformations, and to know that no one individual or institution is alone in pushing these ideas forward—and stumbling a bit along the way. It is important for individuals and organizations to model alternative forms of leadership and organizational thinking in order for our field to grow. Use your voice and your communication channels to share your work in this area, and connect with other organizations supporting similar work.

> We have an extraordinary opportunity at this moment in human history to pause and feel our human connectedness—and to consider how we might respond to both the suffering and the possibility of the moment in ways that create communities of belonging and care. (Osta 2020)

In concluding her essay on leading during the pandemic, Kathleen Osta added these urgent and heartfelt words—words worth holding space for in any and all moments of crisis and uncertainty.

It's time to lead toward a different kind of future, and we've got to get started right now!

REFERENCES

Batliwala, Srilatha. 2008. *Feminist Leadership for Social Transformation: Clearing the Conceptual Cloud.* Creating Resources for Empowerment in Action.

Bell, Jeanne, Paola Cubias, and Byron Johnson. 2017. "Five Insights from Directors Sharing Power." *Nonprofit Quarterly*, March 28, 2017. https://nonprofitquarterly.org/directors-sharing-power-leadership.

Bill Moyers Journal. 2007. "Bill Moyers Talks with Grace Lee Boggs." PBS, June 15, 2007. https://www.pbs.org/moyers/journal/06152007/transcript3.html.

brown, adrienne maree. 2017. *Emergent Strategy: Shaping Change, Changing Worlds.* Chico, CA: AK Press.

Bryant-Greenwell, Kayleigh. 2020. "Waking Up to Wokeness (Actually, 'Woke' is Over, It's Time to Do the Work): An Open Letter to Museum Peers." *Museum as Site for Social Action* blog. https://www.museumaction.org/massaction-blog/2020/6/12/waking-up-to-wokeness-actually-woke-is-over-its-time-to-do-the-work.

Colonna, Jerry. 2019. *Reboot: Leadership and the Art of Growing Up.* New York: HarperCollins.

Cynova, Tim. 2018. "CEO Not (Necessarily) Required." *Medium.* https://medium.com/@timcynova/ceo-not-necessarily-required-4cf4333e2281.

Friedman, Thomas. 2020. "We Need Great Leadership Now, and Here's What It Looks Like." *New York Times*, April 21, 2020. https://www.nytimes.com/2020/04/21/opinion/covid-dov-seidman.html.

Haga, Kazu. 2020. *Healing Resistance: A Radically Different Response to Harm*. Berkeley: Parallax.

Keleher, Terry, Sally Leiderman, Deborah Meehan, Elissa Perry, Maggie Potapchuk, john a. powell, and Hanh Cao Yu. 2010. *Leadership and Race: How to Develop and Support Leadership That Contributes to Racial Justice*. Leadership Learning Community. http://www.mpassociates.us/uploads/3/7/1/0/37103967/leadershipand racefinal_electronic_072010.pdf.

Kocolowski, Michael. 2010. "Shared Leadership: Is It Time for a Change?" *Emerging Leadership Journeys* 3, no. 1.

Mackie, Christopher, and Russell Willis Taylor. 2020. "Thoughts on Co-Leadership: What Do We Think We're Doing?" *Fractured Atlas* blog, February 14, 2020. https://blog.fracturedatlas.org/shared-co-leadership-part-1.

Mont, Simon. 2017. "The Future of Nonprofit Leadership: Worker Self-Directed Organizations." *Nonprofit Quarterly*, March 31, 2017. https://nonprofitquarterly.org/future-nonprofit-leadership.

Osta, Kathleen. 2020. "Leading through the Portal to Claim Our Humanity." *Medium*. https://medium.com/national-equity-project/leading-through-the-portal-to-claim -our-humanity-bf33490ef76c.

Reprojobs. 2020. "Co-Directors in Action: A Joint Interview with All Above All and Reproaction." Reprojobs.com, February 2, 2020. https://www.reprojobs.org/blog/co-directors-in-action.

Stefani, Lorraine. 2019. "Toxic to Transformational Leadership." In *Peace, Reconciliation, and Social Justice Leadership in the 21st Century*, edited by H. Eric Shockman, Vanessa Hernandez, and Aldo Boitano, 177–92. Bingley, UK: Emerald.

Stilwell, Jill. 2019. "When Dual Leadership Works, 1+1=3." *American Alliance of Museums* blog, February 22, 2019. https://www.aam-us.org/2019/02/22/when -dual-leadership-works-113.

Treibitz, Janelle, Tara Dorabji, Favianna Rodriguez, Haleh Hatami, Chucha Marquez, and crystal marich. 2020. *No Going Back: A COVID-19 Cultural Strategy Activation Guide for Artists and Activists*. The Center for Cultural Power. https://backend .ccp.colab.coop/media/pdfs/CCP_Covid-19_3SCNafl.pdf.

Umolu, Yesomi. 2020. "On the Limits of Care and Knowledge: 15 Points Museums Must Understand to Dismantle Structural Injustice." ArtNet, June 25, 2020. https://news.artnet.com/opinion/limits-of-care-and-knowledge-yesomi-umolu-op -ed-1889739.

Weisberg, Robert. 2020. "Museum Leadership for the Rest of Us." *Museum Human* blog. https://www.museumhuman.com/museum-leadership-for-the-rest-of-us.

Wheatley, Margaret. 2017. *Who Do We Choose To Be?* Oakland: Berrett-Koehler.

7

Building a New Model

A Conversation with Lori Fogarty

Being a changemaker and advocating for more radical shifts in organizational structures and leadership requires that we learn from those who have driven change within their own museums. I first visited the Oakland Museum of California (OMCA) back in 2013, having conversations with staff across their institution about the changes taking place to departmental structures, ways of working, and exhibition planning processes. I immediately knew that this was a museum making a commitment to taking risks and making change happen, working to tell the extraordinary stories of California and its people across its collections of art, history, and natural science. Under the leadership of director and CEO Lori Fogarty, who stepped into that position in 2006, OMCA has transitioned from a public–private cultural institution supported by the City of Oakland and the Oakland Museum of California Foundation to an independent nonprofit organization with an innovative new organizational structure. Lori has spearheaded OMCA's efforts to place the visitor at the center of the museum experience and to focus the institution's efforts around community engagement and social impact. Prior to her work at OMCA, Lori was executive director of the Bay Area Discovery Museum and senior deputy director of the San Francisco Museum of Modern Art, so she brings a depth of experience to her ideas around museum change and leadership.

The following conversation with Lori Fogarty took place in January 2020, a couple months prior to the outbreak of the COVID-19 pandemic that led to the closure of museums across the United States and beyond. As OMCA ramped up to make some changes to its building and campus through a major capital campaign, I spoke with Lori about how that museum got to a place of prioritizing its connection with its local community and neighborhood as well as some lessons she's learned about leading change within museums. Some key learnings we discuss in this conversation include:

- Understanding the changes required for a museum to embrace a civic mission and be in service to its community
- Reorganizing the functional and department structures of a museum as a major way to drive internal change
- Working across an organization to build a commitment to community engagement, social impact, and audience evaluation
- Seeing leadership in every area and level of an organization, and developing a leadership advisory team

Mike: There is a famous quote from architect and designer Buckminster Fuller in which he said, "You never change things by fighting the existing reality. To change something, build a new model that makes the existing model obsolete." In the nearly fourteen years since you became executive director at the OMCA, you and your team have been driving forward some fairly significant changes to programs, exhibitions, organizational structures, and the institution's overall connection with its local communities and neighbors— and now a shift in its architecture and physical space. I have been particularly drawn to how this larger museum within a dense, diverse urban area has been able to transform itself to be more community-centered and to increasingly embrace a focus on social impact, social cohesion, and social responsibility, potentially offering up a new model for museum institutions.

I'd love to spend our time together talking a bit more about some of the internal changes at OMCA that have made this evolution possible, the role of leadership in transformative change, and what other museums (large or small) can learn from your challenges and experiences over the past decade. There are more than thirty thousand museums across the United States, which means there are more than thirty thousand museum directors out there leading institutions of all types and sizes. And while I haven't visited them all, I feel like it's probably true that only a small fraction of these leaders are taking the bold steps needed to build meaningful and lasting connections with their local communities (especially individuals and groups that have largely been excluded from museums). I'm curious hearing a little bit from you about what are some of the things that have personally motivated you to be one of those change agents and to dedicate your energies to transforming museums?

Lori: Well, I think part of it is just my personal experience and life experience, and very much my own upbringing, which didn't necessarily position me to be a museum director. I got into the whole museum field because of this belief that museums could make a real difference in the lives of individuals, and eventually in the life of the community. So I think some of it just came from my own value and belief system. At OMCA, some of that inspiration really came from the way the museum was founded.

Early on in my tenure at the museum, our former chief curator of history Tom Frye, who had been there many years, talked to me about the founding director of the museum, Jim Holliday. Jim had recently passed away when I was first starting at the museum, and Tom told me the story about Jim being fired six weeks before the museum opened in 1969 for creating a community advisory committee. So this idea of the Oakland Museum being founded as a museum of the people was very much Jim Holliday's vision. This was at a time of enormous tumult and revolution in the streets of Oakland in 1969. Holliday really had this belief that the museum should be serving its community, and he wanted to bring the community voice into the museum. And when he tried to do that, he was fired by what was then the traditional city leadership in Oakland.

I've taken a lot of my inspiration about what we're trying to do now and tapping into the roots of the museum, and trying to bring out the DNA of what has been the museum's core since its very beginning. I think I've been able to not only get personal motivation but actually motivate a lot of our museum constituents and community by saying this is what we've always been, and we're just trying to realize the vision that was there from the founding.

Mike: Wow, it's certainly interesting to think of a museum director being fired for creating a community advisory committee.

Lori: There were further efforts in those early years to bring in community voice, and there was a lot of tumult—in the city and within the museum—about whose voice would be heard and whose stories would be told. There were very bold and powerful efforts in those early years to still hold up that vision of being a museum of the people.

Mike: Well, it's pretty extraordinary to have a museum founded with that vision, and maybe not so surprising that there were forces acting against that vision right from the start. I think one of the challenges for museums, then and today, is facing the barriers to change and the forces that often pull a museum away from a more community-centered mission. The Oakland Museum was founded fifty years ago amid a tension between these forces, yet so many museums are only now beginning to make efforts toward change. I wonder if you could speak briefly to some of the reasons that museums (and the people leading these institutions) might resist change and are slow to embracing a commitment to social impact.

Lori: That's a really good question. I think some of the resistance to change is certainly based on financial pressures and the ways that museums generate revenue, whether that is public or private funding. There's a perception that the financial pressures make it necessary to focus energy and direct programming to the patrons that are going to support the museum. And part of it has just been that the people that have historically worked in museums, volunteered for museums, or served on the boards of museums have not been representative of the broader population in some of the communities that they reside in. So they are catering to themselves, they're hiring people that are like them, and their boards comprise people who are very similar. And so the motivation, or the even a sense of urgency, around a need to change just isn't there.

I also think that many museum leaders, particularly in art museums, fundamentally believe that social impact is not the intent of museums or the role of their institutions. I have heard many museum directors indicate that their role is to celebrate great art, and that great art is, by definition, relevant, inspirational, meaningful, and timely. They may acknowledge that this "greatness" has historically been defined by the dominant white culture, yet still seem to believe that curators and scholars have the best view on what constitutes great art. And, to the extent that social justice is part of what they present, they indicate that they are "going where the artists go." In other words, they are only presenting great art, and sometimes that art happens to touch on issues of social justice. I, obviously, take some issue with this position, but I want to acknowledge that it is a real and widely held position. It leads to the question: what is the fundamental mission of a museum? Of course, this can differ significantly from museum to museum, so each institution needs to define their mission very carefully in today's context. And I respect that there are other valid missions and lots of variations in between.

As a multidisciplinary museum devoted to California in the heart of Oakland, I believe that our mission requires that we embrace the urgent issues facing our city and state. I believe that in order to be a museum that is embracing a broader civic mission and is truly in service to its community, it requires change at every single level and every dimension of the organization. And that is really, really hard to do.

Mike: I'm really interested in hearing more about some of those organizational changes that have helped advance your mission at OMCA. Can you briefly describe some of those changes that have happened under your leadership at the museum?

Lori: Sure. I would say that after fourteen years, you kind of look in the rearview mirror and see it as a sort of journey in specific steps and moments. I think there have been three real moments of significant change for us. The first was when I first started at the museum. I would say at that point, the museum was not seen as a dynamic resource in the community, but we had received city bond funding for a major reinstallation of our galleries and a renovation to the building. The way the bond language was written required that the reinstallation reflect the changing demographics of California. That process was underway when I began, but we put that whole process on hold and completely rethought how we were going to approach this. And that process took about five years, and pretty radically changed the way we developed exhibitions. Rather than hire an external design firm, we decided to create internal teams to redo these galleries, but with new perspectives and leadership coming to the table. Even to the point of not having the chief curators of the disciplines leading the process, which would have always been the case previously, and would be the case in most museums. So really creating different kinds of processes and different kinds of structures to truly create galleries that were very reflective of our community and that were welcoming, relevant, and accessible to the people of Oakland and the Bay area. That process gave us a little taste of what was possible if we did things differently.

The second moment of internal structural change came in 2010 and 2011. Up until that point, we were a department of the City of Oakland. So making substantive structural change was very difficult because that whole process had to go through city approvals and city budgeting. In 2010, the city was in financial crisis, and the museum took the opportunity to say, "I think we can save the city money, but we need to structure the museum in a really different way." While it took well over a year of negotiations with the city, essentially we became independent of the city. We changed to a structure where we have an unrestricted annual grant from the city and a long-term lease. Along with that shift, we had this opportunity to completely restructure the museum and think through how we could use this opportunity, not just for structural change, but for changing the culture of the organization.

That is when we reorganized into what we call "centers"—six cross-functional, cross-departmental centers. We rewrote every job description, and about 80 percent of the staff actually applied for their positions. It was essentially having people sign up for this institution that you're committed to, with these kinds of values and this kind of a vision. We collectively used this as an opportunity to reinvent, and it was hard. It took a good three or four years to even come out of all of the restructuring.

Our third moment of structural change came through a grant from the James Irvine Foundation as part of their major initiative called the New California Arts Fund. Launched in 2013, this initiative funded performing and visual arts organizations across the state with a mandate to engage low-income communities and communities of color in new ways. That grant came at a perfect point for us because we were emerging from this major restructuring, and doing things in a really different way with a concerted focus on community engagement. The Irvine Foundation funding gave us a lot of support to work in new ways, and not only think about program and audience development but also board and staff capacity building. So it's been each of these steps along the way that has allowed us to move toward our current mandate around social impact.

Mike: Thank you for walking me through this important journey, because I think it's important to understand this history that is a part of the changes you've been able to make happen there at OMCA. I keep going back to that quote that I started out with from Buckminster Fuller about the idea that you never change things by fighting the existing reality. There at OMCA, you had several urgent forces that were propelling you toward many of these massive structural changes. Yet most museums are not faced with these same situations, and therefore have not gone through these more difficult internal, structural changes in the way they work and operate. Looking back on the organizational changes you've led, I'm curious if you could talk about how essential or vital these have been to the overall shift toward social capital, social cohesion, social impact, and neighborhood engagement.

Lori: I would say those changes have been indispensable. I mean, I don't think that we would be able to do what we're doing in terms of programming, audience development, and the way we work with our staff and board had we not made that kind of significant change. And I'm very conscious of the fact that most museums are not required to make that kind of change, or they don't have the type of opportunity we had. I definitely wonder how possible it is for some museums to make the kind of really significant change that I think is required.

When we went through the process of the reorganization in 2010 and 2011, I studied the literature and research around organizational change and why this type of change often fails, including the writings of John Kotter. And the very first step of making a major change to an organization is creating an urgent need, and there was no doubt we had an urgent need at OMCA. I mean, I even felt that with the reinstallation, if we don't do something really different, this museum could die. And when we were faced with these massive financial reductions from the city, unless we really changed the structure, I felt the same way. There was no alternative—the status quo was not going to be viable.

I think that's the difficult part for a lot of museums and museum directors. The ways in which they receive their validation and recognition as well as how they measure success all reinforces the status quo, and therefore doesn't call for the kind of massive change that I think is required. And I do think internal change is required to have external change. It doesn't necessarily need to be the same kind of massive restructuring that we undertook, but I think it needs to be a pretty significant change in ways of working, positions, hierarchies, and ways that we connect with our communities for that change to actually happen.

Mike: That's so interesting to think about. I have worked for several museums that have essentially operated on a traditional status quo model, especially when it comes to the ways in which authority and power live within these institutions. I am so glad you mentioned your efforts to question, rethink, and shift these structures, since I think it is so critical for these conversations about internal change to be elevated whenever possible. The way that museums were set up a long time ago does not necessarily work for the challenges that they're facing today.

Lori: Yes. And I think a lot of where the change often happens is in education departments. The way that a lot of museums have contended with this—especially when it comes to diversity, equity, inclusion, access, and community engagement—is to encourage significant change through their education departments. And there have been incredible examples of work within museums and within communities led by educators.

The challenge, then, is to really move that into the main stage and into the inner workings of museums, especially collecting and exhibition practices. While I've seen more and more museums making some of these changes, it has been really hard to make the change at the fundamental curatorial level and getting other departments at the table with exhibition development.

Mike: I remember visiting OMCA during these changes back in 2013. I had the opportunity to meet with a lot of the staff there, and one of the things that really resonated with me was everyone's commitment to connecting with the museum's neighborhood and local community. There was a lot of energy around thinking differently about the role the museum could play there in Oakland.

So given all of these changes that you've made for almost a decade and a half, I'm interested in where you are now. What are some of the most significant outcomes that you're seeing, and how are these changes benefiting the institution and the local community in terms of social impact and social capital?

Lori: Well, with the Irvine Foundation grant that I mentioned, the mandate has been to focus on engaging low-income communities and communities of color. In this work, we decided to focus our attention on the zip codes immediately surrounding the museum that are among the most economically and ethnically diverse in the region. We did this in a number of ways, both internal and external. This included programming and audience development efforts, and also building a commitment to community engagement into the work of all of our staff and our board. We also made a major commitment to visitor evaluation, which I think is also critical to this process. Around that time, we realized that our audience was changing, our programming was changing, and the way we worked was changing, but to what end? What was the difference we're making?

So we spent a couple of years working with our staff, our board, and experts from the social science field to more deeply understand social impact. After lots of different processes and iterations, we landed on this idea of social cohesion being what we could focus our impact on, in terms of our local community. While it's hard for us to measure community-wide impact right now, we can at least measure our visitors. We're looking at indicators such as do our visitors have a sense of welcome and belonging, do they see their stories reflected, do they see the stories of others, do they have greater understanding and empathy for those stories, and do they connect with people both like them and not like them? And we want to continue to grow and foster these feelings and experiences. Right now, we're doing a major capital project to physically open up our gardens and our building to connect more to the local neighborhood around us, and create that stronger visibility and connection. So that's where we are now.

Mike: Fantastic. I think the work you're doing around measuring social cohesion and social impact is so significant for the field of museums. Thank you for investing in that work.

Lori: Well, it takes a lot of steps to get there. It takes the internal work, the work with staff and the work to truly have your board be reflective of the community. It takes a real commitment to evaluation, so you truly understand who your audience is. For us, I think we've seen a pretty dramatic shift in our audience over these last few years. Last year, 56 percent of our audience were people of color, and that doesn't include school audiences. We've seen a real increase in younger audiences and family audiences. So for us, the social cohesion can't happen if we actually don't have an audience that reflects a broad diversity of people.

Mike: Hearing you speak as an executive director, I'd love to end our conversation talking about some of the things you've learned along this journey about the role of leadership in institutional change and transformation.

Lori: Well, first, I would say that I think that really significant institution-wide change probably doesn't happen without the leader of the organization being committed to it, and leading it. And I think that leadership comes from throughout the organization. I've been continually pushed, prodded, pulled, and encouraged by my colleagues at every level of our institution.

I would say my greatest leadership learning is that it really does take a team. The shift that we made in 2011 with our structure also included creating an executive team of the heads of the centers, and developing a shared leadership model. It has been important for those individual leaders not just to see themselves as advocates of their own specific function or department, but working together toward the same objectives and vision of the organization as a whole. I see a lot of directors having to mediate and navigate between departments or divisions that are trying to protect their own resources, protect their own people, and advocate for their own interests. And that becomes really, really hard for everybody.

I have also learned that leadership needs to come from every level of the organization. In 2011, we created what we call the Lead Team, a leadership advisory team composed of nonsenior staff members who are nominated or self-nominated for a one-year term. They are kind of the culture keepers of the organization, and advocate for better communication and better ways to engage the staff. That team has been indispensable to keeping us honest at the senior level, and really being able to be a platform for employee voice and concerns.

Finally, I would say that I've learned the importance of listening to the community; of bringing in people for every project who are the voices of the topic that we're exploring, bringing in provocateurs as part of that, and people who are going to challenge us to think in different ways. That's become part of our practice—in every project we do, bringing in those perspectives to co-author and co-create the work that we're doing.

Mike: Well, I'm just really grateful to have the time to be able to speak with you about your incredible work leading change at OMCA, and I am so excited to see the new spaces as well as what is in store for the future of your institution and community.

8

Collaborative Leadership That Works

A Conversation with Lauren Ruffin, Molly Alloy, and Nathanael Andreini

Making the shift toward a collaborative or shared leadership model might seem a bit risky for many institutions, yet the benefits of adopting such models are wide-ranging, as discussed in chapter 7 through my conversation with Lori Fogarty. While I was taking a deeper dive into the research on collaborative leadership and co-directorship, I reached out to a few individuals with experience in these types of roles. My first conversations were with Molly Alloy and Nathanael Andreini, who are currently serving as co-directors at the Five Oaks Museum on unceded Kalapuyan land near Portland, Oregon. They have been at the helm of this institution, formerly the Washington County Museum, through a recent period of significant change and rethinking, so I am grateful for their perspectives on leadership as well as on being a changemaker in this field.

Molly is a social change agent and artist who orients their work toward the protection of body, land, truth, justice, and community through tactics of antisupremacist organizational design and integration of art, archive, and movement building. They are the recipient of a Precipice Grant, the Marguerita Mergentime Award for Excellence in Fiber Arts, artist residencies with PLAYA Summer Lake and the Art + Science Initiative, and a founding member of queer curatorial collective First Brick. Nathanael is an artist and youth worker with twenty years of deeply collaborative cultural production experience across the arts, education, and nonprofit sectors. His work is grounded in team development, critical pedagogy, and organizational change. From 2001 to 2008, he was co-founding member of *Sincerely, John Head*, a bicoastal, socially engaged curatorial and artist collaborative. From 2014 to 2016, he founded and co-directed Open Space Performing Arts, a transdisciplinary arts camp for underserved teenagers in South-Central Europe.

Expanding this conversation beyond museums, I reached out to Lauren Olivia Ruffin, who has served as co-CEO of Fractured Atlas, the nation's largest association of artists and creators. Lauren is also a co-founder of Crux; the founder of Artist Campaign School, a new educational program that has trained more than seventy artists to run for political office; and has served on the governing board of Black Girls Code and on the advisory boards of ArtUp and Black Girl Ventures. With twenty years of experience in policy, marketing, fundraising, and strategic planning, she is a frequent speaker on best practices in leveraging immersive storytelling to combat racial and economic injustice. Lauren brings this depth of experience to her perspectives on collaborative leadership and equity in nonprofit organizations.

The following conversation with Molly Alloy, Nathanael Andreini, and Lauren Olivia Ruffin occurred as part of the MuseumNext Disrupt virtual conference in October 2020, and has been adapted for this chapter. Some key learnings we discuss in this conversation include:

- The importance of co-leadership roles in advancing change within organizations, and what it feels like to be in a position of mutual support in these roles
- How and when to make the jump to collaborative leadership models in your organization
- How these changes in leadership structures lead to deeper changes in staff equity and further flattening organizational hierarchies

Mike: The ongoing global pandemic, related economic crisis, and growing demands for racial justice and workers' rights has led to wide-ranging challenges to the traditional structures of museum institutions, including leadership. In many ways, the top-down, hierarchical, solo leadership model adopted by nearly all museums seems incapable of addressing the urgent need to reimagine and reinvent these institutions I am so grateful to be able to have this conversation with all of you, exploring the possibilities of collaborative leadership, co-leadership, and shared leadership, especially at this moment when I believe museums are being asked to reimagine themselves. I want to focus in on why collaborative leadership is important as well as how one can develop more collaborative leadership within one's own institution. Let's begin by hearing more about the collaborative leadership roles that each of you are in now, and the overall context of this structural change within your organization.

Lauren: So with Fractured Atlas, we had a founder transition. Adam Huttler founded the organization when he was nineteen, built it over twenty years, and then brought together a really strong team of four other people to take on that leadership role. At the time when I was hired, I was the last person to join that team. I didn't know Adam was planning to transition, but it wasn't a surprise. The idea of onboarding someone else into managing us sounded daunting, and we had a lot of other things that were really pressing priorities.

And so we did our research and approached the board with a viable option for the organization to maintain stability and to continue to do a lot of the work that we had to do that was really pressing, seamlessly, without having to onboard another executive who was going to bring in new priorities, new ways of doing things. And we already had, in essence, a five-year road map for what we were going to do.

That really made sense to the board. After having known our team for a year or so and seeing how we worked together, they were comfortable with us moving into that space and sharing leadership, sharing power. Because at the core of everything you've talked about, it really is this understanding of accumulating power and holding power at the top of an organization. The arts industry writ large is really built on the backs of unpaid labor, or most certainly, undercompensated labor. It's just a really capitalistic system because you've got folks on boards who are successful capitalists. And I think that trickle-down effect is pretty toxic throughout a lot of organizations in the arts sector.

Molly: Yeah, that's so interesting to hear, Lauren, because there's a lot that I hear that is really resonant with our situation at the Five Oaks Museum, especially this idea of bringing the proposal to the board. There was a moment for the institution, where essentially there was not a path forward, and there wasn't room for the paradigms of power. In our case, with the paradigm of privileging one pioneer narrative over any other examination of history, there was no way for it to move forward and succeed. There was only the option for it to fail. And that failure was happening around us.

But there were things within the institution itself that were having a lot of success, and there was this strong resonance between Nathanael and I and the other staff that were there. We were positioned to carry forward some of the work, in a different way. So we went to the board and presented the idea of a transition. We saw what was working, and a path forward that allowed us to pare it all back down to what's definitely real and what's definitely right. It became just a question of needing to revisit right from wrong, something that had become very confused within our institution, within the industry, and then the country, and then the world.

By being two people, we inherently save ourselves from even the fear of falling back into the same thing, where one person is alone with the burden, alone with the power, unchecked, able to build a lack of transparency around themselves. In order to rebuild the institution in a way that could last longer than just the two of us as individuals being present, we knew that the co-directorship was absolutely necessary. The board was able to embrace that. And this same approach has seeped into other changes and ways of operating for us.

Nathanael: When you can bring a path forward to the power structures that be, whether it's your board or some other executive committee—when you bring a fully seamless approach with the action items and deliverables over a set period—you really just don't leave any room for them to deny it. If you can get proactive with it, all the more power you'll have in enacting it.

Lauren: We were similar in that we both had a void at the top. The organizations that really struggle are when you're really asking people at the top to give something up, possibly for them personally. So either you're going to have to share power, or you're going to have to take a salary cut to bring someone on. It's more fraught for those organizations. And that's when you really get into, how are you studying movement work over generations around what really has happened structurally in a predominantly white industry to really make change, which means, somebody's got to make some hard choices.

So if you're in an organization and you're at the top, the big question is: what are the steps for a seamless transition whereby you're either sharing power, giving up power, or creating a clear pathway for promoting somebody from an underrepresented group, an untapped community to be there with you, or to be at the helm of this organization as you transition across into whatever the new destination for your organization is.

Nathanael: That speaks to me a lot, due to the fact that, right before we proposed this transition, I had been expected to be the interim director of the entire institution. Molly and I had been collaborating unofficially for a while at that point. We both recognized that the structure itself will determine our success as collaborators. We talked a lot of ideas through, but we eventually together decided to propose a co-directorship. What is that like? What does that look like? Let's be living examples, we thought, and try to figure it out.

So I stepped away from a role where I was expected to assume power, and just said to myself "let's not do that." Molly and I worked out ways to adjust this to position ourselves to both be fairly compensated, and to be fair to each other and to the institution. We landed in a great place.

Molly: It's a great point that you raise, Lauren. We both took opportunities that presented themselves instead of having to leverage above ourselves to the leaders that are in those positions for them to enact the change. You're probably right—a lot of the time, that just might be an ask that folks are not going to step up to. I personally think that for any person who's put in this position, their heart, their soul, and their life would flourish way more if they would let themself be in real community with the people with whom they work alongside. It's really painful for people to be isolated in power. And that's part of why it becomes so toxic, and they pass on that toxicity.

So hopefully people are thinking creatively about organizational restructuring as things are having to get reshuffled a little bit right now. As executive director positions become vacant, many organizations are going to have their opportunity to make a shift, and not fill positions one to one.

Lauren: On that piece about sharing the burden, I feel so grateful for sharing leadership with my colleagues for the last six to eight months. Supporting a group of young, creative people through a grieving process that an entire nation is dealing with and having colleagues to share that with was really meaningful. We were able to make really good choices because there were four of us.

There were days when, in particular, I was like, "I can't do it today—I can't show up," and I knew I had three other people there to support me. And we had extra to give to the field that was struggling. The ability to share that actually opened up bandwidth to be of service to other organizations who were struggling with one leader, so we actually ended up taking a slice of ourselves and lending it to other organizations where you did have one person making layoffs.

We're supporting an entire company that's grieving and scared about a pandemic, and there's no way that we could have done that with just one person running the organization. Ultimately, it just made us so much stronger as an organization. Being in leadership just looks so much different than it ever has.

Mike: I definitely agree that a lot of what organizations are being asked to bring to the table in terms of their leadership these days is hard for one person. So, as Molly mentioned, there is an opportunity for a lot of organizations potentially to go down this path of collaborative leadership. I appreciate this conversation, and I want to talk further about the benefits of being in these co-directorship or co-leadership positions.

Molly: There are so many benefits and joys of doing this. We're not just checking in and getting a paycheck at the "Be a Museum Co-Director Factory." This is a job you have to point yourself toward and get into; it's the kind of work that's heart-driven, which means your heart is being exhausted sometimes and also being fed. I think most people, whether they think of themselves as collaborative or not, have probably had that moment where you had a spark of an idea, and in telling it to someone, you hear more of its potential coming out of your mouth, and then they tell it back to you, and you hear it grow in dimension, in impact. You can feel more free to be adventuresome in how you imagine the potential of things. You can cheerlead each other, amplify each others' ideas, and push them to the version that really can have a positive impact faster. When you let yourself be in real, shared work with other people, it's so much more nourishing than trying to keep reminding yourself alone of the benefits. I think it's made me a better human being, and it's definitely made me a better professional.

We talk a lot about binaries, and as a nonbinary person, I often think about the interplay between personal experiences, or my reflections of my journey into my nonbinary identity, and how that implicates the museum, and one of them is the work-life distinction. The idea that you are someone who's not yourself when you're doing your work—that's one of the unhelpful notions that we reject in freeing ourselves to move forward based on what we've really experienced to be the truth. Having a co-director is so integral to even being able to formulate conversations like that because if I was thinking that by myself, it might feel too personal, too out there, too much of a daydream. But when you can chat it through with somebody, it can find legs, and it can take hold and actually become institutionalized. And that's where it starts to be really a different kind of impact.

Nathanael: It's creating a positive feedback loop that you would otherwise only have in your mind, but when you have it with others, in our case in this dual co-directorship, that feedback loop engenders a safe space for sharing, caring, and nurturing each other beyond the work itself. I would absolutely parrot Molly in saying I am by far a better person through this work.

Lauren: I think we're at this pivotal moment as a nonprofit sector where it demands that you question every aspect of how you're working and who's at the table. When you start thinking about all the influences that are happening in the arts sector, whether it's impact investment, artists who are now publishing things independently, community-driven art, or online platforms that are allowing artists to be sustainable, one person in the organization can't manage all that. We have all of these competing forces that as managers and leaders, we're constantly balancing. And somebody's got to be an expert in every aspect of that business if we're going to continue to employ people, if we're going to continue to serve the market that we serve. So being able to stay on top and react and anticipate all of those competing factors necessarily requires more than one person at the helm.

Mike: I think you're exactly right. The pandemic has exposed so many things that existed prior to this moment—problems, issues, and complexities—and I think it has shined a light on the way that leaders are responding to this crisis in different ways. Questioning our accepted models of leadership, and even the way we work, is so vital.

What are some questions you all have for each other about the practice of collaborative leadership?

Lauren: My question is that piece around staff promotion and engagement. Right now, we are really thinking about compensation. And what if we just put all the compensation in a pool and paid it out equally? What are the opportunities for us to really level the playing field for our staff? And I'm wondering if you all are having any of those conversations as well?

Molly: So the day after we get our co-directorship approved, we worked out our pay being less than the previous director, but enough that it was all right for us. Then we started working on staff salary bands in order to have more transparency. We've been officially co-directors since July 1, 2019. We have been able to give our staff three raises in that time. We're basically just pushing as hard as we can to put every inch of vitality that comes back to the museum straight into the staff.

But it's totally not enough. There's no reason why anyone who works with us in this same institution shouldn't have the same opportunity to figure out how to balance their needs as a person with their commitment to the institution. We do know that there are some cautionary tales when you evaporate all of the hierarchy. So we wrestle with this issue. To me, my favorite thing to imagine as of today is that every person would get to determine their own pay. Yet we're totally in the brainstorming phase still.

Lauren: For me, this is the biggest rock I'm trying to climb over right now. How can I justify all my beliefs about equity and wanting people to have everything they need?

Nathanael: I am also interested in asking how these collaborative leadership models inform decolonizing work. Or vice versa, in what way does decolonization inform collaborative leadership? We're a historic museum focused on the pioneer, settler, colonial narratives that we've been having a lot of fun disrupting over the last couple of years. So we're wrestling with decolonizing our actual site, and collective leadership has found its way into that structure by way of trying to decenter authority as much as we can. And we've infused that into our programming.

Mike: This is a really important question. And I think it's important to put that out there before we wrap up, because that's another key part of what we've been talking about—changing the relationship with power and who has it, who should have it, how much of it, what we do with it, and how much we let these Western, capitalistic, and patriarchal norms dictate what that needs to look like.

All of the ideas that you have brought into this conversation point in the direction of taking that leap toward collaborative leadership. I am so grateful to each of you for sharing your insights, lived experiences, and questions that help make a stronger case for adopting shared leadership in practice. These forms of collaborative leadership exist, they work, and they are an essential part of imaging a future for museums that is more equitable, inclusive, and human-centered.

9

Care and Healing

Learning to take better care of and heal each other and ourselves with benevolence could pave the way for the transformation of our communities and planet.

—Pyles 2018, 37

As you show up day in and day out as a force for change and transformation, how are you working in ways that allow you to replenish and sustain yourself? Whether you are the only agent of change working in your institution or part of a growing community of changemakers, it is vital to develop a practice of healing and self-care that can sustain you. After all of the previous chapters on how you can embrace your role as a powerful changemaker, these next pages are dedicated to exploring the importance of developing a practice of care to repair and sustain yourself. And while I know that, for many of us, the idea of caring for ourselves is still a bit "touchy feely" or may simply evoke images of doing yoga at work, developing our own practice of healing and care is an essential way to give attention to the personal, emotional, physical, and spiritual effects on those of us fighting for change within institutions. I encourage you to go through the final chapters with an open mind and an open heart, and begin to bring this mindset of healing and care into your work, your organization, and your community.

This chapter will explore how important is it to take care of ourselves, be mindful, and slow down as part of our work as changemakers, and helps us begin to transform our museums and cultural institutions into healing organizations. The strategies offered at the end of this chapter are just a few practices of care that you can use as you are building your own set of practices to heal and sustain you in your work as a changemaker.

Full disclosure: I actually wrote this chapter while recovering from two separate, back-to-back accidents that forced me to be out of work for several weeks. Up until these accidents, I had been working at breakneck speed, and stress and anxiety had just become an accepted part of the daily grind. In terms of work, many of my priorities and projects came to a grinding halt during my recovery. Not only was I out of the office for a while healing from my injuries, but my slow recovery forced me to put on the breaks, slow down, and meaningfully reflect on the ways I was working—and how I wanted to work going forward. Everyone around me was telling me to "take care of myself," but what did that really mean in a broader sense? Was I taking care of myself before these accidents forced me to slow down? Would I quickly return to the same pattern of overwhelm and overwork as soon as my physical body had healed from my injuries? Did my workplace actually support and honor a culture of self-care and healing, and was I supporting that within my own role as a manager?

A CULTURE OF STRESS AND OVERWORK

Workplace stress in the United States and many other countries has reached unprecedented levels in recent years (and this was before the COVID-19 pandemic hit and the 2020 presidential election season heated up). One study conducted in 2017 found that more than half of workers in the United States felt more stressed than they had one year before, and half of workers reported that the volatile and divisive political climate was their number one stress trigger outside work (Udemy Team 2017). Study after study show that a majority of workers in the United States and in many other countries are not taking their paid vacation time, don't feel they have the support of their supervisors to take paid time off, or simply bring work with them while away from the office. In fact, with the increasing use of laptops and smartphones, the stress of work spills over into our personal lives as we obsessively check email, texts, and social media—another form of stress that exploded with the pandemic and the need to connect with colleagues, co-workers, and family members via video chat services. All in all, an "out of office" automatic email reply means very little today, it seems. We are constantly in a state of looming deadlines and never feeling like we have enough time to do the things we need to do.

This culture of overwork and overwhelm has been frequently glamorized. Numerous studies show that being busy and stressed at work is associated with prestige and status. Complaining about being too busy and desperately in need of a vacation is not only more common these days, but it is increasingly seen as a kind of status symbol (Bellezza, Paharia, and Kienan 2016). I can certainly relate to this workplace culture of expecting and celebrating overwork, especially from managers and leaders in an organization. In our museum institutions and even our professional associations, people are rewarded and celebrated for taking on an overly onerous workload without any regard for their well-being or work-life balance.

If all this stress and exhaustion exists in our average workplace environment, what about in an environment of rapid change? For those working in museums that are in a process of transition and change, you are likely in the midst of something that feels quite messy and unstable: old ways of thinking are being challenged; legacy programs and policies are being questioned; more staff, volunteers, or community members are being involved in decision-making; risks and experiments are becoming more common; new strategic directions reveal previously unspoken disagreements; resistance to change becomes an almost daily obstacle; and we even have moments when we question whether any of this is worth the investment of our own personal time and energy. According to one study by the American Psychological Association (APA), workers experiencing change like this in their organizations are more likely to report chronic stress, physical health symptoms, and increased work-life conflict, among other effects. "Change is inevitable in organizations, and when it happens, leadership often underestimates the impact those changes have on employees," says David Ballard, head of the APA's Center for Organizational Excellence (American Psychological Association 2017).

Overall, chronic exhaustion, overwork, stress, rapid change, global pandemics, and the divisive political climate combined with the cumulative effects of oppression in organizations such as museums are simply grinding people down. The effects of this culture of stress and overload also undermine our ability to effectively and meaningfully center equity, develop sustained partnerships, and build lasting relationships with local communities. To do this work, we need to truly start tending to ourselves.

SAYING THE TERM "SELF-CARE" ISN'T ENOUGH

It is important to recognize that the organizational culture of museums is not set up to address the personal, emotional, and spiritual effects on those fighting for change, leading resistance to patriarchy and racism, and transforming the ways we do what we do. The workplace environment of museums tends to be based in a form of oppressive dominant culture that tends not to prioritize or value capacities for mindfulness, emotional intelligence, and spiritual well-being, often referred to as "soft skills." The regularity of overwork and overload is an ingrained part of this dominant culture that can prevent change from happening in the first place.

How often have you heard the words "take care of yourself" and "be sure to practice self-care" echoed in your museum or workplace? Do you think people mean it? Are you given the time and resources to actually practice care, or given the tools and strategies that can guide you in a healing practice? In her book on self-care for changemakers, scholar and author Loretta Pyles reflects on the ambivalence toward self-care in our predominantly "business as usual" work environments:

> The sad reality is that the attitude of managers and others with power in organizations toward self-care is often complete silence on the issue, rhetoric without action, or meager self-care offerings in an organizational context of business as usual. (Pyles 2018, 15)

Within this dominant culture of whiteness, patriarchy, and European-American values, it can be easy to ignore the layers of privilege involved in the practice of care. Pyles mentions this in her examination of self-care, understanding the criticisms that many of those in the fields of social work and social justice have for a growing industry around care.

> Many change agents are ambivalent about self-care because it has arguably become another commodity of neoliberal capitalism, perpetuating an industry of narcissism, which simultaneously creates greater social disparity and perhaps distracts people from changing the system itself. (Pyles 2018, 16)

If you do a search for #selfcare on Instagram, you can see why there are concerns about the messages of consumerism, luxury, and financial success wrapped up in our society's harmful ideas of self-care.

In her powerful book *Living a Feminist Life*, activist and scholar Sara Ahmed directly addresses the buffer zone of privilege many of us have. As a straight white man, I recognize that I have a lot of built-in support and privilege to fall back on when things get tough or are harmful to me. I was born into a system that was designed to support my success, health, well-being, and education. Therefore, for me and others in positions of privilege, self-care can too easily slip into indulgence, leisure, and vacation. For those living in a system that is not designed to support their well-being, however, self-care can be about survival. To help make this point, Ahmed brings in the often-cited, revolutionary quote from Audre Lorde: "Caring for myself is not self-indulgence, it is self-preservation, and that is an act of political warfare" (cited in Ahmed 2017, 237). In this way, self-care is about looking after oneself—and looking after each other—in a society and system that repeatedly says you do not matter.

In an interview with writer Makiyah Moody about self-care for women of color, Tulaine Montgomery reflected:

> For Black women we are dealing with both patriarchy and racism. We have to navigate both external and internalized bias. . . . Regardless of how you talk, think, or look, recognize that the time you spend nurturing yourself is not a luxury. Don't exhaust yourself into illness before you prioritize self-care. Or if you have already done that, do your best to forgive yourself and build a new set of habits. Value yourself enough to know that you, your ideas, and your inspirations are like the earth . . . precious and finite, so restore and protect your wellness and wellbeing. Self-care is not only for women with disposable income or leisure time, it's for all of us. (Moody 2018)

It is important to recognize the harm and trauma created by racism, sexism, ableism, ageism, and other forms of oppression as we bring care and healing work into our museums. We need to navigate the ways in which white dominant culture has defined professionalism and devalued certain aspects of a holistic healing practice. And we need to cultivate a workplace environment that goes beyond the words *self-care* and more clearly appreciates the work needed to support this practice, provide the space, and develop the tools.

EMBRACING HEALING JUSTICE IN MUSEUMS

During the first half of 2018, I was fortunate enough to be invited to serve as the educator in residence at the Aspen Art Museum. Through this residency, I visited Aspen several times during the winter, spring, and summer months to work with area teachers, meet with staff, and participate in the Aspen Art Museum's final Sustain Retreat—a weeklong gathering focused on reflection, time, and an open exchange of ideas. Aspen is a small town in a rather remote area of Colorado on the Western Slope of the Rocky Mountains. Its population swells with skiers in the winter months and outdoor enthusiasts during the summer months. I quickly learned that it makes an ideal place for visitors to unplug, disconnect from our daily routines, and find some space to reflect—which is why artists, business leaders, thinkers, and musicians have gathered there at the famous Aspen Institute since 1949.

My first visit came in February during peak ski season and lots and lots of snow. I went into these visits with a clear intent to gain some head space and embrace this opportunity to practice self-care, which for me often means reading (books are definitely part of my self-care tool kit). I distinctly remember the first night in Aspen, sitting in my small hotel room while it snowed outside my window, and diving into adrienne maree brown's *Emergent Strategy*. I read this book from cover to cover in one sitting that night, connecting deeply with her ideas of community, spirituality, nature, and holistic transformation. I was drawn to brown's refreshing shift to the positive, her focus on the ultimate importance of relationships, and the way emergent strategy encourages us to recognize the connections among everything that exists around us.

Her writings fueled my interest in this deeper, more personal, and spiritual sense of well-being that I felt museums were largely ignoring. If museum activists and changemakers were interested in bringing social change into the priorities of museum practice, it would be important to connect to the healing practices that made fierce changemaking possible. First and foremost, we have to recognize that working for social change while neglecting ourselves can deplete us. To address this pattern of harm, we need to build a practice of healing. I left my first visit to Aspen with an appetite to learn more about healing justice. As museum professionals, we have a lot to learn from the champions of community organizing and social change.

Healing justice, as defined by scholar Loretta Pyles in her book *Healing Justice: Holistic Self-Care for Change Makers*, is:

> a practice of attention and connection, a way of healing a sense of fracturedness or disconnection that may be a result of trauma, oppressive socio-cultural narratives and practices, or the myriad ways in which humans may lose touch with each other and themselves. It is a practice that asks social practitioners of all kinds to cultivate the conditions that might allow them to feel more whole and connected to themselves, the world around them, and other human beings. (Pyles 2018, xix)

Chicago-based organizer and playwright Tanuja Jagernauth notes that healing justice "recognizes that we *have* bodies, minds, emotions, hearts, and it makes the connection that we cannot do this work of transforming society and our communities without bringing collective healing into our work" (cited in Pyles 2018, xix). Within the framework of healing justice, we are called to care for the multiple dimensions of the whole self: body, mind, heart, spirit, community, and nature. We recognize these dimensions as part of our whole self, and build capabilities such as mindfulness, compassion, and curiosity to nourish these aspects of our self (Pyles 2018, 54–55).

It is important to note that, through this framework, healing and care occur within the context of community, not just one's individual self. As Pyles notes, "self-care becomes just as much about being *in relationship with* and *connected to* others and the world as it is to oneself" (Pyles 2018, 162). We too often think the work of healing is an individual, isolated one. I remember feeling this way as I recovered from my brain injury. It is easy to limit our healing practice to our own body, shutting out the other dimensions of our whole self. Looking back, the three things that played the strongest role in my own healing and recovery were family, community, and nature. In my conversation with museum leader and curator Monica Montgomery in chapter 10, she talks about the importance of community care and what that looks like in practice.

Bringing these practices and this framework into museums may very well be a radical act, but one that I believe is necessary for transformation to take place. It calls on us as changemakers to question organizational norms such as hierarchy, efficiency, and an overemphasis on product and outcomes. It calls on leaders and managers to take action and make sustainable changes in the work environment that support the well-being of workers and our communities. And it calls on us to value relationships at the core of everything we do.

CONNECTING WITH NATURE

Those who contemplate the beauty of the earth find reserves of strength that will endure as long as life lasts. There is something infinitely healing in the repeated refrains of nature—the assurance that dawn comes after night, and spring after winter. (Carson 1998, 100–101)

Across the long history of the human species, we've only been sitting at a desk, in front of a screen, walking on pavement, hearing industrial sounds of machines, or even wearing shoes for a tiny fraction of that time. In her pivotal book *The Nature Fix: Why Nature Makes Us Happier, Healthier, and More Creative*, journalist Florence Williams states:

Over recent decades we have come from dwelling in another world in which the living works of nature either predominated or were near at hand, to dwelling in an environment dominated by a technology which is wondrously powerful and yet nonetheless dead. (Williams 2017, 163)

When was the last time you were somewhere that you couldn't hear the sounds of the human-made world? I honestly can't remember, because even when you're in the middle of a national park you might still hear an airplane fly overhead.

Many people have lost a deeper connection and relationship with the natural world at the same time that our actions are taking a toll on the natural ecosystems surrounding us. We just simply don't connect with nature in slow and intimate ways any more, but a desire for that connection is ingrained in our DNA. As Williams writes:

> We don't experience natural environments enough to realize how restored they can make us feel, nor are we aware that studies also show they make us healthier, more creative, more empathetic and more apt to engage with the world and with each other. (Williams 2017, 4)

Immersing ourselves in the natural environment can be one of the most powerful and effective strategies for care and healing—rebuilding and fostering a deeper connection between ourselves and the natural world.

There is a lot of interesting and compelling research that has been done in the last several years about the positive effects of being in nature on our health and physical well-being. Since moving to the Pacific Northwest, one way I have learned to connect with nature is a technique called "forest bathing." Forest bathing allows us to have an experience where we take in nature through slow, immersive, meditative experiences. We connect with our senses in a deeper way. "Forest bathing is not the same thing as hiking," states forest bathing expert M. Amos Clifford. "The destination in forest bathing is 'here,' not 'there.' The pace is slow. The focus is on connection and relationship" (Clifford 2018, 2). Immersing ourselves in the forest can lower our heart rate and blood pressure, boost our immune system, and increase relaxation and mental clarity. Forest bathing actually even taps into our spiritual well-being and how we identify our whole self by seeing nature as a core part or our being and origin. As Clifford writes, "While we may not be able to get into the forest every week, most of us can find a way to incorporate at least some of the benefits of forest bathing into our lives, through simple ways of continually renewing and deepening our connections to the more-than-human world of nature" (Clifford 2018, xv).

During the summer 2018 MuseumCamp at the Santa Cruz Museum of Art and History, I was invited to lead a forest bathing experience for a group of changemakers. We gathered in a nearby park and shared a series of meditative and mindfulness experiences that allowed us to be present in the moment and connect with nature through all of our senses. I had identified a nearby park that was easy to get to, and we began our experience together by sharing memories of nature from our own personal lives. Then we slowly walked as a group into a small grove of redwoods that towered over us. Our experience together included noticing our surroundings, noticing the sensations and feelings in our body, closing our eyes and listening carefully, touching the trees and soil, and understanding how our senses bring us in contact with the forest. We concluded our experience by sitting in circle under the redwoods, sharing some tea, and having an open conversation about our own restorative and healing practices.

I've had several participants write me since this experience, sharing how important this practice of connecting with nature has become for them.

You don't need a grove of redwoods in Santa Cruz or a deep wilderness forest to connect deeply with nature. It can happen in our backyards, parks, gardens, or anywhere that can bring us in closer to connection to the natural environment. Laura van Dernoot Lipsky, an expert on wellness and founder of the Trauma Stewardship Institute, reminds us:

> We don't have to scale mountains or ride rapids to benefit from being outside, though. Being outside for a few minutes, looking at a tree, and observing the light filtering through leaves can regulate your nervous system and allow you to be more present. (van Dernoot Lipsky 2018, 101)

STRATEGIES FOR CHANGEMAKERS

It is so important for us, as changemakers, to cultivate a capacity for care and healing, and then invest in this mindset by practicing regularly. The following strategies are part of my own personal tool kit and practice, and I'm sure you have some of your own you can share with others. Develop your own care tool kit. Bring these strategies into meetings, one-on-one interactions with colleagues, and your own ways of being in your personal and professional life. Practice these strategies with others, remembering that this work is just as much about cultivating relationships and connections with others as it is about ourselves.

1. Cultivate Mindfulness

Mindfulness can be thought of as a basic human ability to be fully present in where we are, what we're doing, and what we're feeling. Everyone possesses the quality of mindfulness, yet most of us do not take the time to practice it. If you find yourself rushing about your day and bolting from meeting to meeting, find a moment to simply pause and take a breath. Make time to stop, slow down, and regain a sense of calm and clarity. At the beginning of meetings, invite everyone to simple take a deep breath and create a moment of pause before you start. You can also do this in the middle of a meeting or program if things get difficult, emotional, or tense for any reason. While you may get a few eye rolls (I can speak from personal experience on that), it's important that we consistently model a practice of mindfulness and prioritize the well-being of ourselves and the group. This has been even more important during the COVID-19 pandemic as meetings moved online and we were only able to connect through a screen.

Practicing meditation is one of the best ways to build a habit of mindfulness. I know many museum leaders and colleagues who have embraced a daily practice of meditation, sometimes attending group meditation classes or retreats. Meditation can also be a very simple and short strategy you can bring into any moment in our day. For me, the core of any meditation practice is not quieting your mind, but rather recognizing how your thoughts wander, noticing that, and repeatedly bringing your attention back to the present moment. Here is one simple practice that anyone can try while at work or home.

Sitting Meditation

Find a comfortable place to sit and get into a pose where you feel stable and safe. Close your eyes if you are comfortable doing so, and take a series of deep breathes. Begin to disconnect from everything that has been going on during your day, and gently let go of thoughts that might be buzzing through your mind. Notice what your body is feeling—perhaps the texture of the chair, the temperature of the air, the muscles in your shoulders. Continue breathing, and then begin to shift your attention to notice the sounds around you. Take a moment to listen to sounds that might be farthest away from you, and then take time to notice the sounds that are closest to you, maybe even your own body breathing. Refocus on your breathing, and take as much time as you would like staying here. Be as present as you can in your body and in the place you are in.

2. Reclaim Your Time

We all can relate to the constant sense of hurry that has come to epitomize our work culture. In her book *Thrive* (2015), Arianna Huffington examines burnout and exhaustion in the American workplace. She perfectly describes our obsession with time:

> We rigidly schedule ourselves, rushing from meeting to meeting, event to event, constantly trying to save a bit of time here, a bit of time there. . . . We try to shave a few seconds off our daily routine, in hopes that we can create enough space to schedule yet another meeting or appointment that will help us climb the ladder of success. (cited in Pyles 2018, 27)

We lose control over our own time, and become convinced of the scarcity of time. Loretta Pyles calls this a "time famine"—a state of looming deadlines, being constantly rushed, and feeling like there is never enough time to do the things we need to do (Pyles 2018, 27). To resist this culture of hurry, we need to teach ourselves to embrace a practice of slowing down. This means that we control the tempo of our work and life, rather than always having others' schedules and deadlines dictate our time for us. If *we* don't claim our time, someone else will.

Explore Your Relationship with Time

Take a moment to connect with how you use time in your daily routine. What are the factors in your life that have the strongest effect on how you use your time and how you choose the tempo of your day? Give yourself the opportunity to have a schedule that honors you, your family, and your community over externally imposed deadlines and a race to simply "get things done." You might even block in some time each day in your calendar for you—a bit of your day that no one else can touch. You'll thank yourself.

3. Check In with Others

Given that care is a collective practice rather than an individual one, we should be sure to check in and connect with those around us. Make it your mission to check in with co-workers and ask them how they are feeling about work, if they have taken a break, and when they are scheduling in some vacation time. As Pyles suggests, "[B]e a champion for healing justice by engaging in a conversation about the different impacts of stress on people" (Pyles 2018, 216) and discuss how they feel about self-care offerings within the workplace.

Access Check-In

One way to bring this strategy into regular meetings is to practice an "access check-in," a strategy that comes in part from approaches to trauma-informed care. We began doing these regularly in my department at the Portland Art Museum after learning this strategy from Grant Miller, an artist and disability culture consultant we worked with here in Portland. At the beginning of every meeting, simply invite each participate to share a quick personal check-in that shares how they are doing and what they might need to successfully participate in this meeting. For me, this has allowed any group to bring more of our whole selves into our meetings, embrace the different ways of thinking and being across our group in that specific moment, and develop a stronger practice of empathy and listening. You might get some pushback, especially since this may take a bit of time for larger groups, but I believe it is a key part of cultivating an environment of care in the workplace. Take the time to check in, share, and listen to each other.

4. Practice Gratitude

As humans, our brains are actually wired to focus on negativity. To survive, we have evolved to have a sensitivity to danger, harm, and bad news. We're so wired to focus on the negative, in fact, that we need to experience five times as much positive feelings for us to get a sense of balance and equilibrium (Marano 2003). One way to bring a new level of positivity and happiness into our lives is to practice gratitude. "Stepping back to appreciate that we have the sheer opportunity to contribute and have a positive impact in the world can do wonders toward helping us maintain perspective and alleviate overwhelm," writes van Dernoot Lipsky (2018, 84). Gratitude has a significant effect on our overall health both individually and collectively. A key part of gratitude is simply recognizing the positive and the good around us, and overcoming the tendency toward negativity and complaining. Here are some quick strategies you can bring into your daily routine:

- Write down three things you are grateful for at the end of each day. You can have your own gratitude journal near your bed, or even just jot things down on a sticky note before you leave the office. If you get stuck, don't forget to celebrate the people who bring joy into your life. And always remember the little things that make you happy—from the weather outside to a song you heard on the radio while driving to work.
- Share positive experiences and moments with others. At a weekly meeting, ask everyone to share what's making them happy this week. Be sure to extend gratitude to others on a regular basis, and bring the positive into each space you enter.
- Recognize your superpowers and the things that make you awesome. You can do this in a journal, but it can also be fun and meaningful to do this for each person on your team.

5. Get Outdoors

Take some time to get out into the outdoors and find ways to reconnect with the natural environment. Living in the Pacific Northwest, I definitely have the privilege of living close to incredible old growth forests, and it's part of the culture and identity of this place. I certainly recognize that it is not like that everywhere. Yet everyone has some sort of green space nearby. Botanical gardens or nearby parks are amazing places to visit and unplug. Go back to a place to watch how it changes through the seasons.

Take your meetings outdoors for a walk around the block or to a nearby park. Pause for a moment during some time outside and practice some deeper listening—notice the sounds that are closest to you, and the sounds that are farthest from you. Recognize the human-made sounds along with the sounds of the more-than-human world. During the COVID-19 pandemic, we have not been as likely to be gathering for meetings, but you can always change a video call into a phone call, and then participate while you're out in your garden or taking a walk in a nearby park.

One of my favorite exercises in forest bathing is to think of a memory of a tree from your childhood, maybe one you would climb or build forts around. It shows us that all we need is one tree to form a connection. Visit a tree near you and create some sketches, draw some leaves, or make a leaf collection. Touch its bark, wonder how long that tree has been there, and think about the story it has to tell. All of these gestures ground us in the moment and provide us with the sense of connection needed to be present, and sustain us in ways that are essential to being a powerful changemaker.

For me, this chapter on care and healing is so essential and necessary to our efforts to transform our museums. It brings compassion and care to the challenging work of changing institutions and decolonizing spaces. It centers an attention to process rather than just outcomes or product, transforming transactional practices into holistic and human-centered actions.

As individual changemakers and as part of a community of change growing within and across museums, we are constantly influencing the people and institutions around us in small yet extremely meaningful ways. Each conversation we have with co-workers or community members, each planning meeting, each hallway chat, each moment we have to ourselves to reflect on our day—these are all moments when we ultimately get to decide how we are going to bring ourselves into this work. These are all opportunities to be mindful, slow down, embrace gratitude, reduce harm, attend to our whole selves, and plant the seeds for positive change.

Community organizer Grace Lee Boggs wonderfully said, "Transform yourself to transform the world" (cited in brown 2017, 64).

REFERENCES

Ahmed, Sara. 2017. *Living a Feminist Life*. Durham, NC: Duke University Press.
American Psychological Association. 2017. "Change at Work Linked to Employee Stress, Distrust and Intent to Quit, New Survey Finds." May 24, 2017. https://www.apa.org/news/press/releases/2017/05/employee-stress.aspx.
Bellezza, Silvia, Neeru Paharia, and Anat Keinan. 2016. "Conspicuous Consumption of Time: When Busyness and Lack of Leisure Time become a Status Symbol." *Journal of Consumer Research* 44 (1): 118–38.

brown, adrienne maree. 2017. *Emergent Strategy: Shaping Change, Changing Worlds*. Chico, CA: AK Press.

Carson, Rachel. (1965) 1998. *Sense of Wonder*. New York: Harper & Row. Reprint, New York: HarperCollins.

Clifford, M. Amos. 2018. *Your Guide to Forest Bathing*. Newburyport, MA: Conari.

Marano, Hara Estroff. 2003. "Our Brain's Negative Bias." *Psychology Today*, June 20, 2003. https://www.psychologytoday.com/us/articles/200306/our-brains -negative-bias.

Moody, Makiyah. 2018. "Black Women's Self-Care as Self-Preservation." Huffington-Post, July 27, 2018. https://thriveglobal.com/stories/black-women-s-self-care-as-self -preservation.

Pyles, Loretta. 2018. *Healing Justice: Self-Care for Change Makers*. New York: Oxford University Press.

Udemy Team. 2017. "US Study Reveals Rising Stress at Work Driven by Politics, Artificial Intelligence and Pressure to Master New Skills." Udemy, June 6, 2017. https://about.udemy.com/press-releases/workplace-stress-study.

Van Dernoot Lipsky, Laura. 2018. *An Age of Overwhelm: Strategies for the Long Haul*. Oakland: Berrett-Koehler.

Williams, Florence. 2017. *The Nature Fix: Why Nature Makes Us Happier, Healthier, and More Creative*. New York: W. W. Norton and Company.

10

Let's Talk about Community Care

A Conversation with Monica Montgomery

As changemakers, it is important that we take care of ourselves and be part of building an institutional culture of care that reaches outside the walls of our museums through programs, relationships, and partnerships. I have learned a great deal about how museums can better serve and enrich their local communities from Monica Montgomery, a bold arts and culture innovator whom I first met in 2015 through our shared interests in museum change. We've collaborated many times since then, collaborating on projects that bring community service and social justice to the forefront of museum practice—including the transformative Upstanders Festival that I describe in the preface to this book.

Monica uses creativity and narrative as a means of bridging the gap between people and movements. She currently serves as the Curator of Programs and Special Projects for the Smithsonian Institution Arts and Industries Building. As a curator, consultant, and keynote speaker, she uses her platforms to be in service to society. As a museum activist, Monica advocates globally for social justice and relevance embedded in museum practice. She is the founding director of Museum of Impact, a mobile social justice museum, having curated more than forty exhibits and festivals at the intersection of art, activism, and society. Museum of Impact was launched during the inception of the Black Lives Matter movement and partners with local communities in everyday spaces to decolonize museums to bring compelling experiences to people.

I recorded the following conversation with Monica in December 2019, talking about her experiences growing up that led to her deeply held values of care and service that influence her museum practice and activism today, ideas of community care, and some important tips for changemakers and leaders. Some key learnings we discuss in this conversation include:

- Learning to be a changemaker who speaks up, advances a cause, and challenges people to do more
- Listening, collaborating, and developing partnerships as key practices of community care
- Enacting social justice, community services, and social responsibility throughout your museum practice
- Making sure to get out of your office and get to know your local communities and what's happening in your neighborhood

Mike: One key value and idea that has emerged in my own practice, and that I feel is vital for museum practice overall, is care. How do we care for ourselves, and extend that care to our colleagues and our communities? While many people might focus solely on "self-care," the idea of "community care" is something you've talked about and brought into your own practice.

And I remember distinctly back in October of 2017, you visited Portland for the MuseumNext conference and to produce the Museum of Impact's "Museums Respond" exhibition. You were presenting a session at that conference, and I'll always remember this moment. You had everyone in the room close our eyes, and you asked us to think about and visualize the people we care about most. After a few moments, we opened our eyes and you challenged us to think about that feeling of care and how we might bring that into our own work with communities or within our own institutions. That moment really stuck with me because I felt museum professionals, myself included, were talking a lot about empathy, but really this idea of care is more radical. In that talk, you defined community care as "an architecture of practice to honor our community, centering advocacy, empathy, and social responsibility."

So I wanted to spend our time together talking more about this idea of community care within the context of museums. I would like to start by just asking where valuing that kind of idea comes from for you. When was that something that became important to you and what were some formative things for you in developing those ideas?

Monica: Well, definitely it's great to share about the concept of community care. While it is not a concept that I invented, it is one that I've spent some time speaking on and practicing in museum work and beyond. I think a combination of things have led me to think that institutions can be stewards of enacting and manifesting community care. Growing up as an only child in New York City in the 1980s and seeing the widespread poverty, the need, the lack, and homelessness—that always touched me as a child, and made me just react to the needs of humanity differently.

I always tell this story about when I was with my dad when I was young. We would walk down the street, and I wanted my dad to give a dollar or change to every homeless person we saw, no matter what. I'd say "Hey, Daddy, this guy needs something. Hey, don't overlook him. Dad, do you see him underfoot?" And my dad was like, "We can't give to all of them." "Why not?" I'd respond, because they all were clearly out there for a reason. I just couldn't stand to think of a human being in the streets who is either hungry or distressed or in need of medical care, and people just walk by and do nothing. That idea was unconscionable to me, and I always thought that even if no one else cares and everyone's going about their daily life, I care.

And over the course of my youth, I did a lot of work in Girl Scouts and work with homeless people themselves, getting to know them, asking them what sort of circumstances prompted them to be in this situation, and asking how I can serve their needs. So homelessness, particularly as a humanitarian crisis and social justice issue, has really affected me and made me have a different lens on humanity. I wasn't, and I'm still not, the type that can just walk by and see someone suffering and think, "Well, someone else will handle that." I want to personally get invested.

There's always been a heartstring pulling from me, especially when it comes to people and causes that affect people. I think also there's books I've read and movements I followed. For example, humanitarians Craig Kielburger with Marc Kielburger wrote the book *Me to We: Finding Meaning in a Material World* (2006). They talk about service projects and living to help others and enrich the community. And so formative texts like this have helped. I am a Christian and I still go to church and practice Christianity and there's certainly a love your neighbor as yourself component that I've always taken very seriously and actualized.

In essence, I think a lot of my foundational background has made me a really empathetic, caring person. In terms of museums, my entry to the museum world was as a unpaid volunteer/intern who had to struggle to be seen, to be visible, to have my work be something that could be considered seriously. There was a real strong curve of trying to get from being at the bottom of the pyramid to a place where my words were even regarded enough to be considered for a stage. So I always said to myself in those times of economic scarcity that one day when I do get a chance to speak and people care about what I'm saying, I'm going to always represent for others like myself who have been disregarded, downtrodden, and overlooked. I'm going to make sure to never forget this feeling and always speak truth to power for those that don't have the voice, don't have the platform, don't have the money. So I guess all of that has stuck with me, has shaped me, has formed me and I never forget those experiences. I always think about community care.

Mike: I really appreciate you talking about where these ideas and values come from in your life experiences. I think too often we're looking for skills and expertise that are learned from a graduate program or in our professional work, yet we don't recognize and value those skills that we learn from navigating our own experiences throughout life. Recently, I've really appreciated making sure that we're reconnecting with where our values come from even before we got our first job or maybe decided to go to college.

You spoke about how your life experiences have shaped how much you value caring for others and making sure that you're using your position and your voice to care for others. I'm curious how practicing community care started to become something that you felt the need to passionately advocate for within museums. Because by the time I first heard you speak at conferences many years ago, you had already become such a strong and unapologetic voice for social justice and community care as well as an advocate for transformative change in museums. I'm really curious about what your thought process was around deciding to be that passionate advocate for these ideas of care and community care within museum practice.

Monica: Honestly, it's because I've always had the notion that I'm never really going to wait for anyone else to articulate or do what I think is necessary to advance a cause, a movement, and an industry. In all my speaking, I attempt to look around for best practices and for people that are doing what I'm referencing, and make sure to give them credit and highlights. If I don't see enough of it happening, then let's speak about what we can do to evolve in this way. Here's what we can do, here's why it's important, here's some that have done it and there's more of us that can.

I just never feel compelled to sit and wait and hope that someone will catch on. I think that part of being a thought leader is to challenge people to think about what more we can be doing, how can this work can come into our organizations, and how can we use these ideas in action and not just talk about them at conferences. So from that lens of not waiting for validation, not waiting for approval, not waiting for someone to do it first, but speaking it into existence, I've led and jump-started many things, from social justice pop-up museums and movements for equity and diversity to gatherings and groups and hashtags. I feel that someone has to be that lightning rod to do that work and keep everyone focused on what we can do with this power we have without getting comfy or too self-congratulatory.

Mike: I'm always super interested in how museums actually start to embrace this kind of mindset of care into their practice as an institution. What are some of the ways that museums can start to grow and embrace this idea of community care? What are some practical things that you've seen even work as a museum starts to make this part of their change?

Monica: I think just finding points to collaborate and involve those people who are outside the institution, people who don't necessarily hold the power but whose opinions, voices, and perspectives we value and need to get involved with elements of the running of the institution. So whether that's an advisory board, a teen council, community curation, or having frequent town halls and meetups in this space, the more community-minded our museums are, the better.

And this can be hard to do depending on the structure. I know that many smaller museums and institutions are very community-minded and some were founded by community members. However, there are large institutions that weren't necessarily set up that way, so it would take some doing, decolonizing, and reimagining. I think that community members outside the institution who don't necessarily hold the power in the decision-making should be involved, consulted, considered, and really centered in these processes.

Another great way to embrace community care is using the museum as a platform to enact social justice within your community. Through my own work at institutions, I have planned activities for the Martin Luther King Day weekend of service, for example. And I think it can be revolutionary to use the museum as a space that says, "Let's be about service and let's see how we can serve others or use this as a platform."

When we embrace community care, we're centering an architecture of empathy, advocacy, and social responsibility to honor our humanity. Empathy, on a basic level, is caring for one another, putting yourself in someone else's shoes. Advocacy is something we all can do, and there are many ways to advocate that are nonpartisan. I think that as many museums as possible should sign up to be election polling places and serve as active sites for voter registration. And social responsibility is not just social justice in a vacuum, it's really about how we care for one another and hold ourselves accountable for one another's welfare. So just like any other place where human life takes a front seat—a hospital, a park, a school—I think museums can also be involved in that work.

Mike: A lot of the things that you've mentioned are definitely things that I'd love to see museums take on more and more. Envisioning the museum as a platform for community service is something that many of us see resonate with our own institutions; yet we desperately need to grow and expand our institutions' capacities to support such service projects. This type of work needs to be supported and valued from across an institution and its leadership, and not only within the education departments of museums. It is so important to hear museum leaders like yourself and others begin to support this type of practice and drive it forward.

And I love really centering this idea of collaboration and partnership with community. Through my own practice, I have found that one of the key aspects of building more community collaboration and community care has been trying to build trust. While I see a lot of institutions doing work that's being labeled "community partnerships," I just don't feel like many are focused on building (or rebuilding) trust. It feels really important to me that museums work to build trust with members of the community that really haven't ever been given a reason to trust your institution in the past.

I wonder if you could speak a little bit to that trust formation process. What are some ways museums can think about that? Because I think all the things you've talked about are so powerful and I think museums can make a big mistake by jumping too fast to trying to do a bunch of projects and programs with communities that haven't yet been given a reason to trust especially a large institution that has been very exclusionary for a long time.

Monica: That is definitely a great point and I would say that I'm also on a learning curve with building trust between institutions and collectives, groups, and individuals. I think we have to realize that there's been a lot of trauma on the part of individuals, groups, and collectives in their interactions with any large institution. There have been breaches of trust, there have been hard feelings on both sides, and it's hard for either side to understand the perspective of the other.

Now more than ever, perhaps, institutions like museums are desirous of engagement and wanting to do things to promote equity and create opportunities for partnerships. So I think it is incumbent upon these institutions to prove their worthiness, their good intentions, and their righteous acts to the community. And it's important to be transparent about everything.

So if it's that a museum is desiring a relationship, one way to do it potentially is to announce that there is an interest in forming relationships with community groups. And I think starting really slowly is so important, and having conversations with all the stakeholders. When I have had my partnership teams approach individuals, groups, and collectives, I always have them do more listening than talking. We always begin by asking, "What does partnership mean to you?" Just that alone, that simple question, is revolutionary. I think asking that upfront and throughout is so key, and helps everyone involved get clear on expectations.

Mike: Yeah. I really appreciate what you said about listening and also asking what partnership means for everyone involved. In many cases, we all enter into partnerships and collaborations with a set of assumptions and expectations, yet we might not take the time to talk openly about these and actually shape a partnership together. I am really learning the value of this in my own practice. I think it's a step that a lot of institutions skip, so I really appreciate that you mentioned this because I think it does make a big difference.

Monica: And I'll just say that when I write a memorandum of understanding for partnerships, I have a sentence in there about bringing our highest and best intentions, good vibes, and a positive agenda to the partnership. I find it helpful to include any and all expectations, and I have a whole section on shared accountability. I try to get really technical about it. Not to say that it always ensures good outcomes, but having things on paper can really help clarify things.

Mike: Yeah, clarity is such an important part of all of this. There is definitely a specific set of skills, practices, and ways of being that are core to this type of community partnership work, and I think these practices emerge from the people doing it. I find that many of the people that are building relationships in the strongest ways are working with smaller museums and cultural institution rather than with the big, more traditional institutions. So I think there's a lot of learning and a lot of listening that needs to happen among practitioners.

Monica: I also think there is something to be said for learning the fine art of what a partnership looks like between institutions. It is a great way to build community and enact community care, and I think that institutions that stick together can do better. So these same skills can be used to strengthen our alliances with other institutions which also makes us better, stronger, and more empathetic.

Mike: I am so grateful for you and many other museum leaders right now that envision museums as embedded within their communities, truly community hubs that are part of these local networks and alliances. It helps build museums into part of the collectives within our communities that are making these better places to live. Whether it's in urban, suburban, or rural communities, I think museums can really be a part of that change.

Given where you are in your leadership work now, I'm curious if you would have any one thing to say to other people who are entering a leadership position at an institution about how they might really bring this idea of community care to the center of an organization and as part of the work that they're driving forward.

Monica: Sure. I would recommend that people really get out of the office and get to know what's happening around you, in the neighborhood, on the block, in the community, in the city, in the region. Really get invested and involved with what goes on beyond your institution. In doing so, you'll meet amazing potential partners, community leaders, and future friends as well as start to see your role as more expansive—an organism in a greater ecosystem. So the life of a city, a county, a space involves art and culture but also expands beyond arts and culture. And how can arts and culture play a meaningful part in the life of that area? Understanding the whole life cycle of a citizen, a space, or a region really enhances your lens for leadership. So you can then get your organization the information it needs to really be of service to the citizens of your region, and ensure that you are a welcoming, warm community hub that is attempting to meet the needs of the citizens.

So it's getting outside the walls, getting to know what's happening in the area, meeting other leaders, and then connecting with your team and seeing how we are an asset and how we can help. I think that gives a great framework for enacting community care.

REFERENCE

Kielburger, Craig, and Marc Kielburger. 2006. *Me to We: Finding Meaning in a Material World*. New York: Touchstone.

11

Propelled by Love

The moment we choose to love we begin to move against domination, against oppression. The moment we choose to love we begin to move towards freedom, to act in ways that liberate ourselves and others. That action is the testimony of love as the practice of freedom.

—bell hooks, "Love as the Practice of Freedom" (2006, 250)

One of the things that we really have to do that is completely radical is utterly invest ourselves in love and to continue to practice that. . . . Love that changes, love that confronts, love that holds you, love that allows you to make mistakes but only within love.

—Reverend angel Kyodo williams, *Radical Dharma* (2016, 145)

[I]f we want to change something, we must first begin to love it.

—Lama Rod Owens, *Love and Rage* (2020, 152)

Throughout life, there are those moments we experience that just stick with us. It can often be something quite small—and probably unnoticeable to others—yet it resonates deeply within us for some reason. It connects with our heart in a deeper way. These experiences become part of our own personal and professional growth as we reflect upon them months and even years later. I want to end the learning journey of this book by recognizing a simple moment that keeps coming up for me—a tiny spark that has fueled so much of my own thinking about the changes we need to see happen in museums and the ways we need to approach that process of change.

In November 2016, less than a week after a presidential election that left so many feeling numb, confused, raw, and angry, I traveled to New York to attend the MuseumNext conference, a gathering of more than five hundred museum leaders and professionals from around the world. I was fortunate enough to be facilitating the conference's first-ever Museum Social Action Project with Monica Montgomery, a leading thinker in museums and the founding director of the Museum of Impact, the world's first mobile social justice museum. Monica and I had decided that it was important to get conference attendees outside the walls of the conference venues and out into the local communities, learning more about the exceptional work happening on the ground when it comes to social impact. We planned out a day with the Laundromat Project (LP) at their Kelly Street Initiative in the South Bronx.

Launched in 2005 to make art accessible and relevant in New York City neighborhoods where people of color reside, the LP advances artists and neighbors as change agents in their own communities. Bringing art making, arts programming, and leadership development to everyday community spaces, the LP works to make sustained investments in growing a community of multiracial, multigenerational, and multidisciplinary artists and neighbors committed to societal change. Their artists and staff work to amplify the creativity that already exists within communities by using arts and culture to build community networks, and enhance the sense of ownership in the places where people live, work, and grow. Their Kelly Street Initiative had launched in 2015 in the South Bronx, transforming a two-bedroom apartment into a thriving creative community hub and artist studio space.

On that sunny morning in November, Monica and I gathered with a small group of museum professionals and leaders from across the United States and parts of Europe to visit the Kelly Street space, learn about what drives the work of the LP, and think about ways to bring this sense of community ownership and neighborhood engagement into our own museum practice. We were joined by Hatuey Ramos-Fermín, the LP's director of programs, who gave us a tour of the building and community garden and led a few discussions that explored the idea of a neighborhood as well as strategies for engaging with local residents. Sitting inside the ground-floor level of this apartment-turned-community arts space, we learned about the origins of the Laundromat Project and its broader work. Hatuey shared the values of the organization, including creativity, place, community . . . and *love.*

Love? As a value for a nonprofit organization? (Or any organization, for that matter?) Working in museums, I was used to institutional values being things like accountability, education, intellectual inquiry, innovation, or excellence—the types of words that don't necessarily get your blood pumping or get you out of bed in the morning. But love? That felt like such a powerful, emotional human value—a concept we didn't talk much about around the senior leadership tables at museums. I was trained to think that love was far too "touchy feely" to be a serious, professional value driving an organization's mission and work. But there it was, projected on the wall of that apartment in the South Bronx. Love.

I remember raising my hand before Hatuey moved on to the next slide, and simply asking how it was that love came to be added to this list of the LP's values. I just hadn't seen that before, and I was honest about that. I recall him talking a bit about their discussions that led to these values, and how much their team felt the need to bring a radical idea like this to the forefront. Something that elevated their work above just arts programming or community engagement. Love has continued to be a central driving force for the LP, and they describe their current value, "Be Propelled by Love," in this way: "We value love as a radical and essential act of power and protest to create the kind of world we all deserve to live in."

That moment, and that decision to make "love" an organizational value, has stuck with me ever since that day at the Kelly Street Initiative. And while no museum that I've personally worked for myself has ever considered bringing an idea like love into its core values, I have increasingly brought it into my own practice as a changemaker and into my work with others around me. Despite the frequent resistance, I've even had some conversations with colleagues about the role of love in museum practice, and how we can start to open up more to this idea that is very much needed these days, especially through the work of changing museums.

Back during summer 2019, I visited my colleagues in the Learning department at the Tate Modern in London, where they have explicitly identified love as a core value and "the fundamental value underpinning what we do" (Pringle 2014). In an article about how love manifests through programming at the Tate, head of research Emily Pringle frames the importance of bringing an emotional and intellectual component to their practice, quoting Paulo Friere: "We must dare, in the full sense of the word, to speak of love without fear of being called ridiculous, mawkish, or unscientific" (Pringle 2014). I've been consistently energized by those who genuinely embrace love in their practice and understand the profound systemic changes needed in museums to bring this deeply human value to the center. As I write these words at the conclusion of this book—this very personal journey for me—I strive to enact Friere's words and dare to speak of love. I encourage you, as a changemaker and as a leader, to do the same.

In today's culture, we generally have a very limited definition of *love*. As Friere suggested, the idea that love is important is often mocked; it's seen as Hallmark-ish and soft. In places like museums, when we speak about love, we're often dismissed as being too sentimental. There is a pressure to focus on intellectual discussions and ideas of the head, ignoring the importance of our heart. It's almost entirely unheard of to have ideas like love enter into strategic planning sessions or meetings of the board of trustees. Where is the courage needed to change this? We need to be those changemakers and leaders who are willing to stand apart, believe in something bigger than themselves, and invest in love as a core practice and way of being.

In his collection of sermons published in 1963 titled *Strength to Love*, Dr. Martin Luther King Jr. wrote about the necessary and transformative power of love, and what it means to have the courage to love. King wrote, "Love is the most durable power in the world. This creative force . . . is the most potent instrument available in mankind's quest for peace and security" (King 1963, 41). Writer and activist Darnell Moore defines love as "that illuminating energy that removes the barriers that otherwise separate us" (Moore 2017). This is the love that can lead the radical transformation needed for museums and other organizations to become more human centered, community centered, and equity centered. This is the revolution needed right now for our institutions to turn toward community care and healing. As adrienne maree brown writes in her pivotal book *Emergent Strategy*:

> When we are engaged in acts of love, we humans are at our best and most resilient. The love in romance that makes us want to be better people, the love of children that makes us change our whole lives to meet their needs, the love of family that makes us drop everything to take care of them, the love of community that makes us work tirelessly with broken hearts. (brown 2017, 9)

If you finish this book and only take away one idea into your practice, I hope it is the deeply human act of love that is at the utmost core of our work to transform museums into more generous, welcoming places that center community, equity, connection, and care.

This final chapter is not a stopping point, a concluding statement, or a culminating moment. Rather, I see it like a comma—a moment of pause for each of us to reflect on our own journey as changemakers thus far, and then to focus our energies on that next step into the future filled with courage, humanness, and love. I recognize that I am writing these words amid the grief, pain, and uncertainty of a global pandemic that has changed all of our lives in ways that we will never forget. At this moment, the call for museums to radically reinvent themselves has never been more urgent or more necessary.

I invite you to take this pause, give yourself some space, and work toward taking actions (even just something small) that lean toward bringing more loving-kindness into your work, your practice, and your life. In remembering her husband, James Boggs, and his passionate and revolutionary call to love during the Civil Rights Movement, Grace Lee Boggs writes:

> Love isn't just something you feel. It's something you do everyday when you go out and pick the paper and bottles scattered the night before on the corner, when you stop and talk to a neighbor, when you argue passionately for what you

believe in with whoever will listen, when you call a friend to see how they're doing, . . . when you never stop believing that we can all be more than what we are. In other words, Love isn't about what we did yesterday; it's about what we do today and tomorrow and the day after. (Boggs 2012, 96–97)

What if love, above everything else, was the core value that steered the radical change needed in museums today? What if each of us made a commitment to bring love into action through our personal and professional work, today and tomorrow and the day after? What if we created an environment or a space in which love could flourish? What would that look like for you? For your community? What would you need to change about yourself and your own practice to make this happen?

My deep desire for change in museums comes from a place of love that has grown over the past two decades through countless experiences of togetherness, connection, pain, sharing, learning, and healing—both within and outside the walls of these institutions. My love for museums is entirely based on the people that have come together and shared experiences with each other—and with me—because of these places. I've seen museums be a place where people come together during tragedy, when they feel they have nowhere else to go. I have locked arms with others in mourning after tragic events like the Pulse nightclub attack in June 2016; the mass shooting in Las Vegas in October 2017; and remembering and celebrating the lives of Michael Brown, Quanice Hayes, Christopher Kalonji, and others killed by police in our own communities. And I will never forget that day in May 2017 when hundreds of people came together at the museum after the horrific attack on the MAX train here in Portland. On that day, the museum became a space of emotional connection and support—an act of solidarity against violence and hate. I know what museums look and feel like when they begin to live up to their full potential as openhearted spaces of care and humanity, and my demands for change come from this place of love. Museums everywhere have the potential to take action, dismantle their own systems of oppression, build a more equitable future, and be those places that bring people together and change people's lives.

A different future is possible, and it is up to us to make this happen together.

> Each new hour holds new chances
> For new beginnings.
> Do not be wedded forever
> To fear, yoked eternally
> To brutishness.
>
> The horizon leans forward,
> Offering you space to place new steps of change.
>
> —Maya Angelou, *On the Pulse of Morning* (1993)

REFERENCES

Boggs, Grace Lee. 2012. *The Next American Revolution.* Berkeley: University of California Press.

brown, adrienne maree. 2017. *Emergent Strategy: Shaping Change, Changing Worlds.* Chico, CA: AK Press.

hooks, bell. 2006. "Love as the Practice of Freedom." In *Outlaw Culture: Resisting Representations.* London: Routledge.

King, Martin Luther Jr. 1963. *Strength to Love.* New York: Harper and Row.

Moore, Darnell. 2017. "You Are Not My Leader If You Don't Love Me." *Huffington-Post*, December 6, 2017. https://www.huffpost.com/entry/you-arent-leader-if-you-dont-love_b_9229394.

Owens, Lama Rod. 2020. *Love and Rage: The Path of Liberation through Anger.* Berkeley: North Atlantic Books.

Pringle, Emily. 2014. "Art Practice, Learning and Love: Collaboration in Challenging Times." Tate Research Publication. https://www.tate.org.uk/research/research-centres/tate-research-centre-learning/working-papers/art-practice-learning-love.

williams, angel Kyodo. 2016. *Radical Dharma: Talking Race, Love, and Liberation.* Berkeley: North Atlantic Books.

Index

About the Author

Mike Murawski is an independent consultant, change leader, author, and nature lover living with his family in Portland, Oregon. He is passionate about transforming museums and nonprofits to become more equitable and community-centered. After more than twenty years of work in education and museums, Murawski brings his personal core values of deep listening, collective care, and healing practice into the work that he leads within organizations and communities.

Since 2011, he has served as founding editor of ArtMuseumTeaching.com, a collaborative online forum for reflecting on critical issues in the field of museums. He is also co-producer, along with La Tanya S. Autry, of Museums Are Not Neutral, a global advocacy campaign aimed at exposing the myth of museum neutrality and calling for equity-based transformation across museums. Murawski is grateful to have served as a contributor to the Museum as Site for Social Action (MASS Action) initiative supporting equity and inclusion in museums and as First Wave Project Advisor for the OF/BY/FOR ALL initiative helping civic and cultural organizations grow of, by, and for their communities.

In 2016, he co-founded Super Nature Adventures LLC, a creative design and education project based in the Pacific Northwest that partners with parks, businesses, and nonprofits to develop content and design interpretive resources aimed at expanding access and learning in the outdoors and public spaces.

Murawski has served as the director of learning and community partnerships for the Portland Art Museum, director of School Services at the Saint Louis Art Museum, and coordinator of education and public programs at the Mildred Lane Kemper Art Museum at Washington University in St.

Louis. He earned an MA and PhD in education from American University in Washington, DC, focusing his research on educational theory and interdisciplinary learning in the arts.

When he is not writing, drawing, or thinking about museums, you can find him out on long trail runs in the forests and mountains of the Pacific Northwest.